The Book of
Painted Quilts

Handpainted Quilts & Other Home Accessories

When fabric goes under the brush of talented decorative artists, the results are simply stunning. The painted quilts (and quilted items, such as table runners, wall hangings, and pillows) along with companion pieces on "non-fabric" surfaces create a visual feast!

You can see the talent on display—every stroke of the brush and every stitch combine perfectly to convey an overall cohesive feeling to each piece.

The Decorative Arts Collection Museum is grateful to all the artists who were involved in this project. Your painting, piecing, and quilting talents made this a collection of masterworks.

Thank you to everyone who worked so hard to make this possible —

- Trudy Beard
- Ronnie Bringle
- Judy Diephouse
- Cynthia Erekson
- Cindy Gensamer
- Jo Sonja Jansen
- Jamie Mills-Price
- Peggy Stogdill
- Chris Thornton-Deason
- Gloria Ware
- Sandy Yarmolich
- Cheri Blocker
- Lynne Deptula
- Donna Dewberry
- Peggy Harris
- Audrey Hydrick
- Andy Jones
- Sherry Nelson
- Bobbie Takashima
- Time Treasured Quilts
- Mary Wiseman

THE DECORATIVE ARTS COLLECTION MUSEUM

The Decorative Arts Collection Museum was created in 1982 for the purpose of collecting, preserving, and displaying fine examples of decorative painting. The Decorative Arts Collection Museum houses works of artistic, historical, and contemporary significance. Additionally, the museum provides exhibitions and educational programs which increase public appreciation and understanding of decorative painting, including its heritage, methods, and techniques.

Lend your financial support to the museum by becoming a Friend of the Museum.

Visit the museum online. Learn more about the artifacts in the collection, shop in the museum shop, and see past exhibitions.

The Decorative Arts Collection Museum
www. decorativeartscollection.org
650 Hamilton Ave SE
Suite M
Atlanta, GA 303012
404-627-3662

The Book of
Painted Quilts

Handpainted Quilts & Other Home Accessories

Published by

All American Crafts, Inc.
7 Waterloo Road
Stanhope, NJ 07874
www.allamericancrafts.com

Publisher: **Jerry Cohen**
Chief Executive Officer: **Darren Cohen**
Product Development Director: **Brett Cohen**
Art Director: **Kelly Alberston**
Copy Editor: **Mary Ellen Bruno**
Editorial Advisors: **Linda Heller & Donna Koenig**
Quilting Diagrams: **Rory Byra & Cate Tallman-Evans**

The Discovery Magazine for Decorative Painters
www.paintworksmag.com

www.quickandeasypainting.com

Printed in USA
©2009 All American Crafts, Inc
ISBN-13: 978-0-9789513-8-2
ISBN-10: 0-9789513-8-7
Library of Congress Control Number: 209932437

Contents

Cascade of Roses Quilt

Trudy Beard

Lush pink roses create a romantic ensemble!

Materials
- 6¼ yards of white tonal fabric
- *Plaid* FolkArt Fabric Paint (Brush On): Berry Wine, Coastal Blue, Fuchsia, Hauser Green Medium, Lavender, Lemon Custard, Magenta, Red Violet, Wicker White, Yellow Citron
- *Royal & Langnickel* Majestic #12 shader (Series 4150), #10/0 script (Series 4585), ¾" glaze wash (Series 4700)
- *Miscellaneous:* foam core board (for under painting area), masking tape, paper towels, white pastel pencil, white plastic trash bags

Preparation

1. Launder, dry, and iron the fabric. Do not use fabric softener or spray starch.

2. Cut the fabric into three, 25" x 75" panels. Lay the panels on a large, flat surface. Using a white pastel pencil, draw diagonal lines across each panel.

3. Cover the foam core board with a white plastic trash bag, and secure with masking tape. Lay fabric over the prepared foam core.

4. *Note:* Rather than use a pattern, the shapes of the roses may be freehanded at the initial block-in stage of the painting, with leaves and filler flowers added as you paint the roses.

Painting

Note: Refer to the Worksheet on page 9 as paint.

Light pink roses

1. Dip the ¾" glaze wash brush into water and blot lightly. Load the brush with a brush mix of Magenta + a touch of Wicker White. If the paint is too wet, it will run; if it's too dry, it won't move easily. Experiment to get the right consistency.

2. Create the rose shapes with this mix. Note that slightly irregular shapes make the most interesting roses. Corner-load same brush with a touch of Berry Wine, and shade the center of the rose, the right side, and the lower edges. Clean the brush in water and then squeeze it dry.

3. Load the ¾" glaze wash or #12 shader with a brush mix of Magenta + a bit more Wicker White. Add the middle values to the rose with a short, flat stroke under the center, and then add strokes from the left outer edges.

Darken the brush mix slightly by adding more Magenta and stroke the shadow side.

4. When the rose begins to dry, add the highlights with Wicker White + a touch of Magenta. Adjust the highlights and shadows, if needed.

5. Add accent colors on the shadow side with a brush mix of Coastal Blue + a touch of Wicker White *or* with Lavender + a touch of Wicker White.

6. Apply small irregular Berry Wine dots with the tip of the #10/0 script. Dry-wipe the brush, and highlight the dots with Yellow Citron. Blot off the excess dots with your fingertip.

Deep pink roses

1. Dip the #12 shader into water and blot lightly. Load with a brush mix of Magenta + Fuchsia, and paint the deep pink rose shapes. Corner-load the dirty brush into Berry Wine, and shade the center of the rose center, the shadow side, and the lower edges. Clean the brush in water and squeeze dry.

2. Brush mix Magenta + a touch of Wicker White, and paint the middle values. Follow the technique described for the light pink rose in step 3 above.

3. Stroke the highlight using the #12 shader and a brush mix of Magenta + a bit more Wicker White. Adjust highlights and shadows, if needed.

4. Finish as instructed above in steps 5 and 6 for light pink roses.

Leaves

Note: Paint the large leaves with the ¾" glaze wash and the medium and small leaves with the #12 shader.

Painted panel

1. Dip brush in water and blot lightly. Brush mix Hauser Green Medium + a touch of Berry Wine, and stroke the leaves. While the leaves are still damp, corner-load the dirty brush with Berry Wine, and apply shading to the leaves at the widest part of the leaf and down the center. Clean the brush in water and squeeze dry.

2. Begin adding middle values using brush-mixed Hauser Green Medium + Coastal Blue, Hauser Green Medium + Lemon Custard, or Hauser Green Medium + Yellow Citron. Load the brush and blot lightly, then stroke with a light touch.

3. Highlight the leaves where necessary. Dip the brush in water, blot lightly, and load with scant amounts of brush-mixed Coastal Blue + Lemon Custard and Coastal Blue + Yellow Citron. Add Wicker White to the mixes to further highlight.

4. Dip the #10 script into water, and using any of the mixes listed in step 3 above, line the center veins and stems.

5. Adjust shadows and highlights. Add accent colors, mostly in the shadow areas, with Coastal Blue, Lavender + a touch of Wicker White, Magenta + Wicker White, Red Violet, or Red Violet + a touch of Wicker White.

6. Loosely outline the leaves with Hauser Green Medium + a touch of Berry Wine. Thin the paint with water for finer linework.

Filler flowers

With the corner of the #12 shader and very little pressure, dab in subtle filler flowers of Red Violet, Red Violet + Lavender, Lavender, Lavender + Coastal Blue, or any combination of the above + Wicker White.

Tendrils

Load the #10/0 script with water and dip into a brush mix of Hauser Green Medium + Yellow Citron + a touch of Wicker White, and apply the tendrils. *Note:* Practice fine lines on your palette, holding the brush as far back on the handle as you can, and moving your entire arm, not just your wrist.

Finishing

Air-dry the painting for 24 hours, then heat-set with a dry iron and a press cloth. Hand- or machine-wash on cool after 72 hours.

Cascade of Roses Worksheet

Quilting

Quilt designed, pieced, and quilted
by **Cindy Gensamer**

Skill level: Beginner/Intermediate
Finished quilt size: 72" x 72"

Materials

Note: Yardage is based on 42" wide useable fabric.

- Three painted panels trimmed to 22½" x 72½"
- ½ yard each of six assorted pastel or batik print fabrics
- 80" x 80" piece of backing fabric
- 80" x 80" piece of batting
- Thread in colors to match fabrics
- Template plastic
- Basic sewing and rotary cutting supplies

Cutting

From each of the six different prints, cut:
One 3½" x 42" strip; recut each strip into twenty-four 1½" x 3½" pieces
Enough 2½" bias strips to equal 350" when sewn together for the binding (lighter shades of fabric were used in the featured quilt)

Assembly

Note: Use a ¼" seam allowance throughout. Sew all pieces with right sides together and raw edges even, using matching thread.

1. Referring to the **Quilt Layout Diagram**, sew seventy-two 1½" x 3½" assorted color pieces long sides together to make one long strip. Press seams in one direction. Repeat to make a second pieced strip.

2. Stitch the three painted panels alternately together with the two pieced strips to complete the 72½" x 72½" quilt top.

3. Layer the quilt top right side up on top of the batting and the wrong side of the backing. Baste the layers together and quilt as desired.

4. Using the patterns provided, trace the corner scallop and side scallop onto template plastic and cut out neatly. Referring to **Diagram 1**, position the corner template on one corner of the quilt top and trace. Align the side template against the corner template and mark the top edge. Trace the side template a total of three times and align with the corner template on the opposite corner of the quilt top. Repeat on the remaining sides. Cut neatly along marked line and baste ⅛" in from the edge of the scalloped border. This will keep the layers from shifting when the binding is sewn on.

5. Sew the 2½" wide assorted bias strips diagonally together to make one continuous strip. (See *General Quilting Directions.*) Press seams open. Fold the binding strip lengthwise in half with wrong sides together and press. Align the raw edges of the binding strip with the scallop border on the front of the quilt, and leaving a 3" tail, begin stitching at the top of one scallop. At the bottom of a curve, stop

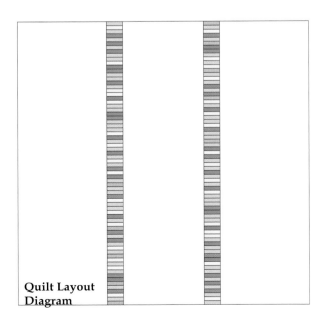

Quilt Layout Diagram

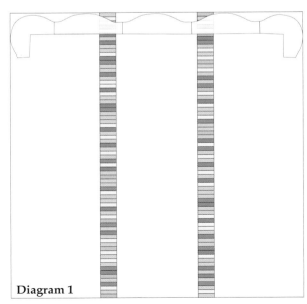

Diagram 1

with the needle down, lift the presser foot, pivot the quilt and binding, then continue sewing, taking care not to stitch in any pleats. Continue around the quilt, easing the binding around the curves, being careful not to pull or stretch the binding as you sew. When within 3" of the starting point, stop stitching, then cut the binding end so it overlaps the beginning by about 4". Cut the end diagonally and turn the cut edge under ¼". Lay the beginning inside the diagonal end and finish sewing the binding to the quilt. Fold the binding to the back of the quilt, over the raw edges of the quilt sandwich and covering the machine stitching. Hand-stitch the binding to the back of the quilt.

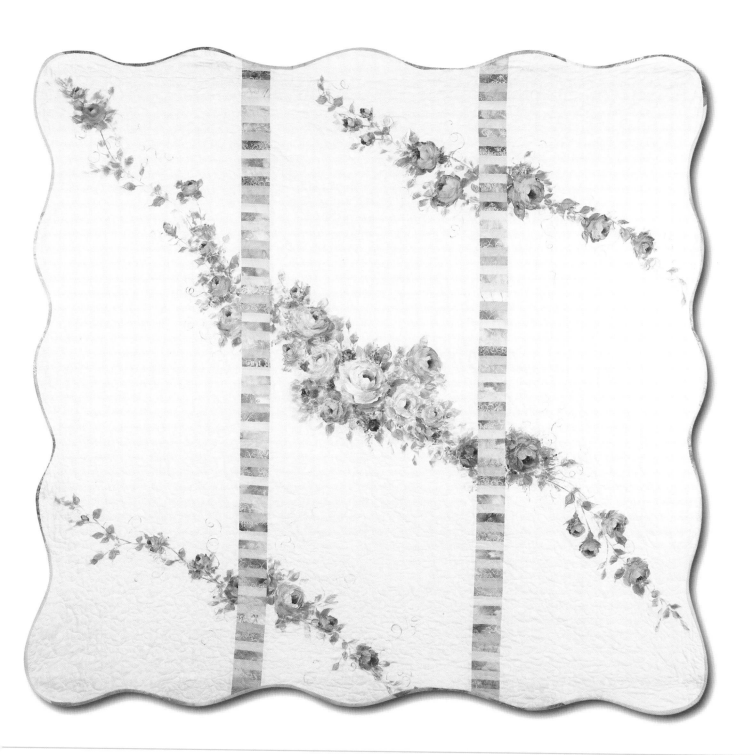

Rose Chair Seat

Cascade of Roses Quilt Companion Piece

Preparation

1. If necessary, remove particles of rust and old paint with a wire brush. Wipe down with a damp cloth, and let dry.

2. Spray with primer and then paint, following all manufacturers' instructions. When dry, lightly sand to smooth. Sand more on some areas to replicate worn paint. Wipe with a damp cloth, and let dry.

3. *Note:* Rather than use a pattern, irregular rose shapes may be freehanded at the initial block-in of the roses. Add leaves and then filler flowers as you paint the roses.

Painting

Acrylic rose technique

Do *not* use water to paint roses with acrylics. Instead, moisten the brush with FolkArt Blending Gel. Blending Gel allows the paint to dry slower, and when added to the accent colors, creates transparent strokes of color. Follow the steps on the Worksheet on page 9 and use the same techniques used for fabric painting, but substitute Blending Gel for water.

Light pink roses

1. Dip the ¾" glaze wash brush into Blending Gel and blot lightly. Block in an irregular rose shape with a brush mix of Magenta + a touch of Warm White. Corner-load the same brush with a touch of Burnt Carmine, and shade the center, the right side, and the lower edges of the rose. Clean the brush in water, and squeeze dry.

2. Load the ¾" glaze wash or the #12 shader with a brush mix of Magenta + a bit more Warm White. Add the middle values to the rose with a short, flat stroke under the center, and then add strokes from the left outer edges. Darken the brush mix slightly with more Magenta, and stroke the shadow side.

Materials

- Old ice cream parlor chair (or surface of choice)
- *Plaid* FolkArt Acrylics: Lavender, Light Fuchsia, Magenta
- *Plaid* FolkArt Artists' Pigments: Aqua, Burnt Carmine, Hauser Green Medium, Turner's Yellow, Warm White, Yellow Citron
- *Krylon* Indoor/Outdoor Primer, White
- *Krylon* White Spray Paint, matte finish
- *Royal & Langnickel* Majestic #12 shader (Series 4150), #10/0 script (Series 4585), ¾" glaze wash (Series 4700)
- *FolkArt* Blending Gel
- *J.W. etc.* Right-Step Clear Varnish, matte or satin
- *Miscellaneous:* paper towels, sanding block, soft cloth, wire brush

3. Add highlights with Warm White + a touch of Magenta. Paint the final highlight with Warm White. Adjust highlights and shadows. Add accent colors to the shadow side with a brush mix of Aqua + a touch of Warm White *or* with Lavender + a touch of Warm White.

4. Add small, irregular Burnt Carmine dots with the tip of the #10/0 script. Dry-wipe the brush, and highlight the dots with Turner's Yellow and Yellow Citron.

Deep pink roses

1. Dip the #12 shader into Blending Gel and blot lightly. Following the same techniques as used for the light pink roses, block in the rose shapes with Magenta. Corner-load the dirty brush with Burnt Carmine, and shade the center, the shadow side, and the lower edges of the rose. Clean the brush in water and squeeze dry.

2. Brush mix Magenta + Light Fuchsia, and paint the middle values.

3. Stroke the highlight using the #12 shader and a brush mix of Light Fuchsia + a touch of Magenta. Add the final highlight with a mix of Magenta + Warm White.

4. Adjust highlights and shadows. Add accent colors to the shadow side with brush mixes of Aqua + Warm White *or* Lavender + a touch of Warm White.

5. Add small, irregular Burnt Carmine dots with the tip of the #10/0 script. Dry-wipe the brush, and highlight the dots with Turner's Yellow and Yellow Citron.

Leaves

Note: Paint the large leaves with the ¾" glaze wash brush and the medium and small leaves with the #12 shader.

1. Dip the brush in Blending Gel and blot lightly. Brush mix Hauser Green Medium + a touch of Burnt Carmine, and stroke the leaves. While the leaves are still damp, corner-load the dirty brush with Burnt Carmine, and shade the leaves at the widest part of the leaf and down center. Clean brush, and squeeze dry.

2. Begin adding middle values with a brush mix of Hauser Green Medium + Yellow Citron and Hauser Green Medium + Yellow Citron + Warm White. Stroke the mid values with a light touch.

3. Dip the brush in Blending Gel and blot lightly. Highlight the leaves with brush mixes of Yellow Citron + Warm White + a touch of Aqua and Hauser Green Medium + Turner's Yellow + Warm White.

4. Adjust shadows and highlights. Add accent colors, mostly in the shadow areas, with brush mixes of Lavender + Warm White, Magenta + Warm White, and Aqua + Warm White.

5. Loosely outline leaves and add center veins with Burnt Carmine + Hauser Green Medium. Thin the paint with water for finer linework.

Filler flowers

With the corner of the #12 shader, dab in Lavender, Lavender + a touch of Burnt Carmine, Aqua + Warm White, and Lavender + Warm White filler flowers.

Tendrils

Load the #10/0 script with water, and dip into a brush mix of Hauser Green Medium + Yellow Citron + a touch of Warm White, and apply the tendrils.

Finishing

1. Allow the painting to dry overnight.
2. Varnish with two or more thin coats of matte or satin varnish. Allow adequate drying time between applications.

Grandmother's Flower Garden Lap Quilt

Peggy Stogdill

The inspiration for these designs was a delightful patchwork quilt my grandmother made from recycled aprons and housedresses in the 1930s!

Materials
- 1½ yards of white tonal fabric (for painted floral squares; reserve remaining for quilting instructions)
- *DecoArt* Americana SoSoft Fabric Acrylics: Avocado Green, Brown, Buttermilk, Cadmium Orange, Cadmium Yellow, Crimson, Dark Burgundy, Dark Chocolate, Fuchsia, Hauser Dark Green, Lamp Black, Lavender, Mediterranean Blue, Peaches 'n Cream, Primary Blue, Primary Yellow, Red Pepper, White
- *Winsor & Newton* Regency Gold Golden Taklon #2, #4, #6, #8, and #10 synthetic short bright (Series 510), #0 synthetic round (Series 520)
- *Loew Cornell* La Cornielle Golden Taklon #10/0 Jackie Shaw liner (Series JS)
- *Chacopaper Co., Ltd.* Super Chacopaper, Blue
- *DecoArt* Americana SoSoft Transparent Medium
- *Masterson Art Products* Sta-Wet Palette
- *Miscellaneous:* backing surface (such as stiff cardboard), fine-line marker, 1" foam brush, sharp #2 lead pencil, palette knife, paper towels, stylus, tape, tracing paper, cloth or spray mister bottle

Preparation
1. Prepare fabric according to fabric paint manufacturer's instructions.
2. Cut three 12" x 42" strips, then recut into eight 12" squares
3. Trace the design from the Pattern Section onto a piece of tracing paper with a fine-line marker. Transfer the pattern using Chacopaper and a stylus. If desired, use a light pencil to reinforce tiny detail lines which may dissolve on contact with medium, paint, or water.
4. Tape the fabric square on the backing surface.

Techniques
- Unless otherwise indicated, always apply paint and Transparent Medium with a short bright brush of appropriate size for the area.
- Before applying paint, always completely basecoat an area (up to the pattern lines) with Transparent Medium until it is wet, but not soggy, and has no dry spots. Lift off any excess with the brush before painting.
- It is usually best to finish each item, working wet-on-wet, before going on to the next. *Note:* If paint begins to dry before completion, allow the item to dry thoroughly, then reapply medium and continue to strengthen shading, etc.
- Work shading and tints into the Transparent Medium base. Sideload with small amounts of paint, pinchwipe the brush clean, and blend the color until it gradually fades away into the light and highlight areas. In most instances, the unpainted fabric forms the light/highlight areas.
- Apply paint first to darkest areas, and to lighter areas when the brush is nearly empty. Reload as necessary. Pull paint into very light areas during blending, rather than apply fresh paint.
- Strengthen the shaded areas while Transparent Medium base is still wet. Paint each successive application of color in a slightly smaller area than the previous area (this is referred to as pyramiding the values).
- When blending, if the paint isn't moving as it should, work a bit of Transparent Medium into the bristles of the blending brush.

Painting
Note: Parentheses ( ) around a color in a mix means to use less, or a touch, of this color. Refer to the Worksheet on pages 19 and 20 for the following steps.

Brown-eyed Susan
1. *Petals.* Apply Primary Yellow to the base and to the tip of a petal. Work the paint side to side, not lengthwise. Blend, leaving the center free of paint. Pull a little paint along the edges of the petal if not defined by overlapping petals. Blend more Primary Yellow on edges, if needed.
   Blend Brown shading at the base of the petal

and narrow shading on petals that turn under or are beneath another petal. With the chisel edge of the brush, pull a few subtle vein lines of color up from the base of the petal. Let dry.

If not enough fabric highlights are showing through, reinforce with drybrushed White.

2. *Flower center.* With a sideload of Brown, paint the crescent shape in the upper part of the center and larger crescent on the left side. Blend until it fades into unpainted light areas. Sideload with Dark Chocolate and pyramid darker shading within both shaded areas. Blend.

Paint tiny lines around the center with Dark Chocolate and a liner. When dry, loosely paint Buttermilk pollen dots with a round brush.

3. *Warm leaf.* Shade with Avocado Green at the base of the leaf, the center vein gully, and randomly on outer edges and tip. Blend, leaving light areas unpainted. Pyramid secondary shading with Avocado Green + (Lavender) at the base and tip of the leaf. Reinforce edges with Avocado Green, if needed.

With Lavender + (White), tint the edge on the left from the center of the leaf downward toward the dark shading. When dry, paint the center vein with White and a liner. Once dry, drybrush a small amount of White to strengthen highlights, if needed.

4. *Cool leaf.* Paint in the same manner as above, using (Hauser Dark Green) + Avocado Green + White. Reinforce with the same color at the base of the leaf.

5. *Small leaves.* Paint some of the leaves with the warm leaf mixes and some with the cool leaf mix. While wet, paint the center vein with a liner and the initial mix used on each leaf.

Stems and small filler leaves (all designs)

1. *Stems.* With the chisel edge of the brush, paint the outer edges Avocado Green, with color a bit wider on the left edge. Slightly blend the paint lengthwise. Leave fabric exposed to form center light area. Apply and blend Avocado Green across the stem where it goes under objects.

2. *Small filler leaves.* Paint with a pastel mixture of Avocado Green + White + medium. Add a bit more Avocado Green to the mix, and paint the center vein with the liner brush.

3. *Linework and filler leaf stems.* Use the liner and a light pastel mix of Avocado Green + White + medium. For best results, use fresh paint and move the brush slowly.

Bachelor buttons

1. *Bottom flower.* Blend Primary Blue into the base and the tip of the petal, leaving light areas

free of paint. Pull a little paint along the outside edges of the petal if not defined by other petals. Pull a few vein lines with the chisel edge of the brush.

Sideload the brush with Primary Blue + (Lamp Black). Pyramid darker shading, mainly at the base, but occasionally on tip, of the petals. Blend. Tint an occasional petal tip or edge with a dirty brush and Lavender or Mediterranean Blue. Paint Lamp Black stamens with a liner brush.

2. *Remaining bachelor buttons.* Paint center flower as above, but add White to the initial Primary Blue shading. Add more White for the top flower.

3. *Calyx.* Sideload with Avocado Green and paint the shaded crescent on the left, a more narrow application on the right, and the shadow across the top. Blend, leaving the center unpainted. While wet, paint the stem. Blend slightly where calyx and stem join. Pyramid darker shading with more Avocado Green at the top of the calyx and within the crescent on the left.

Load just the edge of the #2 short bright, and paint the upside-down V-shapes on the calyx. Begin at the top and work toward the bottom, offsetting the V-shapes. Only portions of the V-shapes may be visible as they turn around the sides of the calyx.

4. *Leaves.* Paint with the warm and cool greens from the Brown-eyed Susan leaves. Apply paint at the base and tip of each leaf, then pull a bit of color along the sides while blending. Reinforce color, if needed. Tint two or three edges with a dirty brush of Lavender. Pull a center vein with the chisel edge of a bright brush.

Zinnia

1. *Petals.* Sideload the brush with Crimson, and then shade and blend as before. Use more Crimson for darker areas. Use the chisel edge of the brush to pull a few vein lines of color out from the petal base. Pyramid Dark

Burgundy shading at the base of most petals, anywhere petal separation is needed, and beneath the flower center.

2. *Flower center.* Paint and blend the small shaded crescent in the upper portion with Dark Burgundy. With the small round brush, layer tiny teardrops of Cadmium Yellow + Dark Chocolate in the remaining larger portion of the center. Begin with strokes around the outside, extended a bit over the outer edge. Aim strokes toward the small oval shape in the upper portion of the center. Layer more strokes with Cadmium Yellow, and then add a final layer with Buttermilk.

3. *Warm leaf.* Apply and blend Avocado Green. Reinforce leaf base with Avocado Green + (Dark Burgundy). Tint on right edge with a dirty brush of Crimson. While wet, pull out side veins from the center vein area with the chisel edge of a brush. When dry, line the center vein with White.

4. *Cool leaf.* Paint in the same manner as the warm leaf, but with the colors used for the cool Brown-eyed Susan leaf.

Gaillardia

1. *Petals.* Paint and blend Red Pepper at the base, and occasionally on an edge, of a petal. Paint the tip of the petal Cadmium Orange + Primary Yellow. Blend, keeping the band quite narrow. Pyramid Dark Burgundy shading at the base of most petals, and anywhere needed for petal separation. Blend, leaving light areas free of paint. Pull veins with the chisel edge of the brush from the petal base toward the tip. When dry, reinforce light areas with Buttermilk, if needed.

2. *Flower center.* Shade inside edge of circle with a sideload of Brown. Blend, leaving center unpainted. Shade a wide crescent shape on the left with Dark Chocolate. Continue with a narrow band around the remainder of the outer circle. Blend.

With the corner of the bright brush, loosely dab a mix of Dark Chocolate + Lamp Black + Dark Burgundy on the outer circle, dabbing a bit heavier in the area of the crescent on the left. Loosely dab Dark Chocolate spots on the inner circle with a round brush.

When dry, loosely dot orange pollen around the outer edge of the center using a round brush

and Cadmium Orange + Primary Yellow. Paint little green lines around the center with a liner and Avocado Green. Highlight a few with a tiny stroke of Buttermilk.

3. *Leaves.* Paint in the same manner as the Brown-eyed Susan leaves, but with secondary shading at the base of the warm leaf on the left, using Avocado Green + (Dark Burgundy). Tint with a dirty brush of Red Pepper.

Cosmos

1. *Top flower.* Apply Fuchsia + White at the base of the petal and to most areas of the outer edges. Blend, leaving some edges devoid of paint. Occasionally use Lavender on an edge instead of the Fuchsia mix. Blend, leaving the fabric exposed to form light areas. Pull color with the chisel edge of a brush to create veins. Reinforce with more Fuchsia, pyramiding the color at the base of the petal and creating a value change on the edge. Pyramid tiny areas of Dark Burgundy for final shading.

2. *Remaining cosmos.* Paint in the same manner, but lighter. Add more White to the Fuchsia + White mix. Use a bit less paint and eliminate final Dark Burgundy shading.

3. *Centers.* Dab Cadmium Yellow dots with small round brush, avoiding highlight area in upper right. Shade dark crescent on left with Dark Chocolate dots. With a dry round brush, dab back and forth between the colors to blend.

4. *Leaves.* Sketch leaves, a few at a time, with medium. For the center cluster, apply and blend just enough Avocado Green to define the leaves. Keep them quite light. Repeat with the cool leaf mix for the remaining leaves.

Pansies

1. *Two back petals.* Apply and blend Lavender. Vary width of paint on outer edges. Leave some edge areas of large petals unpainted, as they will be defined by the petals behind them. Apply darker shading where the

petals go under others, and here and there on outer edges to create ruffles.

Tint with a dirty brush of Fuchsia on the lower left of each back petal of the top flower, and on the lower right of the larger back petal of the bottom flower.

2. *Side petals.* Apply and blend Lavender + White. Again, leave some areas on the edges unpainted, and with no paint at the base of the petals. Reinforce shading with more Lavender.

Using the liner, apply Lamp Black linework.

3. *Front petals.* These are similar to the side petals, but paint a triangle of Primary Yellow at the top of the petal and blend slightly across the bottom edge. On the front petals, begin dark lines at the bottom edge of the yellow triangle. Using a clean, dry, small bright brush, tap the top end of each line where it meets the Cadmium Yellow triangle to settle it into the paint underneath.

When dry, place a Lamp Black + Lavender teardrop at the top of the petal. With a liner, outline each side of the top of the petal with a tiny comma stroke of White.

4. *Pansy bud.* Shade with Lavender.

5. *Leaf.* Paint first shading with Avocado Green, and second, darker shading with Lavender. Tint with Lavender + White.

Tulip

1. *Petals.* One petal at a time, apply and blend Cadmium Yellow shading, and second shading of Brown. Sideload a brush with Red Pepper and paint some edge areas of the petal, varying the width. Blend slightly; then, holding the brush parallel to the surface, walk a bit of the red color into the yellow, creating soft streaks that follow the petal growth direction. Pinch the paint out of the brush between a paper towel often. Vary the streaks in length, width, and value. Deepen the shading in some streaked areas with Crimson. Paint stamens Avocado Green, and highlight with White. Create center veins with the liner and White.

2. *Tulip leaf on the right.* Sideload with Avocado Green, and shade bottom of leaf, tip, and here and there on outside edges. Blend, pulling some color onto empty places on the edges. Paint darker shading at the leaf base with

Avocado Green + (Crimson). With the chisel edge of the brush, pull some paint up to create a center vein. Pull finer side veins, parallel to the center vein.

3. *Tulip leaf on the left.* Shade with Hauser Dark Green + Avocado Green + White. Reinforce with Hauser Dark Green + Avocado Green. Tint on the lower left with Avocado Green.

Orange daisy

1. *Petals.* One petal at a time, paint a Cadmium Yellow band approximately ¼" wide where the petals attach to the daisy center (except on the foreshortened petals in the front where it won't be visible). Blend slightly. Sideload with Peaches 'n Cream. Paint tips and edges of petals that won't be defined by underneath petals. Blend, pulling lengthwise veins. Paint the area where the front petals attach to the center with Peaches 'n Cream. With Cadmium Orange, apply a secondary, brighter shading, and reinforce the color on some petal tips, a few edges, and at the base of most of the foreshortened front petals. Blend, again pulling a few veins. Tuck in darkest areas with Dark Burgundy, mainly on underneath front petals and underneath petals in the upper right.

2. *Center.* Dot with Dark Chocolate and a round brush. Use varying pressures for dots of different shapes and sizes. Begin in the darkest areas of the center, painting the light area once the brush unloads. Reinforce the dark crescent with dots of Dark Chocolate + Burgundy.

3. *Leaves.* Paint the first shading on the warm left leaf with Avocado Green. Leave some edge areas unpainted, pulling a bit of color into them when blending. Reinforce a few areas with more Avocado Green. Reinforce the leaf base with Dark Burgundy. Tint with Peaches 'n Cream. Pull side veins with the chisel edge of the brush.

Paint the cool leaf on the right, following previous cool leaf instructions. Add Peaches 'n Cream tints.

Finishing

When the paint is dry, remove any remaining blue transfer lines by dampening with water on a cloth or in a spray mister bottle.

Grandmother's Flower Garden Worksheet

Quilting
Quilt designed, pieced, and quilted
by *Cindy Gensamer*

Skill Level: Beginner/Intermediate
Finished Quilt Size: 37" x 34"

Materials

Note: Yardage is based on 42" wide useable fabric.
- Eight painted floral panels trimmed to 11" x 11"
- Reserved white tonal fabric
- Thirty-five 5" charm squares or scraps of assorted 1930's print fabrics
- One fat quarter (18" x 22") or ¼ yd. of six different color pin dot print fabrics (in the same shades as the 1930's prints)
- 3" x 40" piece of backing fabric
- 43" x 40" piece of batting
- Thread in colors to match fabrics
- Template plastic
- Awl or ⅛" hole punch
- Basic sewing and rotary cutting supplies

Cutting

Note: The patterns for Pieces 1 through 3 are located in the pattern envelope and include the ¼" seam allowance. Trace the patterns onto template plastic and cut out neatly. Use an awl or large needle to make holes at the seam intersections (as marked on each pattern.)

From each of the eight 11" x 11" painted flower panels, cut:
One of Piece 1 with the painted motif centered; then, on the wrong side of each piece, mark the points of the seam intersections (through the hole made in the template)

From the reserved white tonal fabric, cut:
Two of Piece 2; then, on the wrong side of each piece, mark the points of the seam intersections
Enough 2½" x 42" bias strips to equal 180" (for binding)

From each of the different color pin dot fabrics, cut:
Five of Piece 3; then mark the points of the seam intersections on the wrong side of each piece

From the charm squares or assorted 1930's prints, cut:
Thirty-five 4½" squares

Directions

Note: Use a ¼" seam allowance throughout. This quilt presupposes a basic knowledge of piecing set-in seams. (This type of seam is used when a continuous straight seam is not an option. Stopping and pivoting is necessary to sew a piece into an angled opening between other pieces that have already been joined.) Stitch all pieces with right sides together and raw edges even, using matching thread. Sew from marked point to marked point; do not stitch out to the raw edges of the pieces.

1. *Top and bottom hexagon row.* Following **Diagram 1**, sew four 4½" squares and three Piece 1 hexagons alternately together to make one row. Repeat to make a second row.

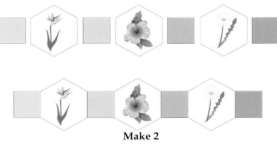

Make 2
Diagram 1

2. *Middle hexagon row.* Stitch three 4½" squares and two Piece 1 hexagons alternately together as shown in **Diagram 2**. Sew a Piece 2 to each end.

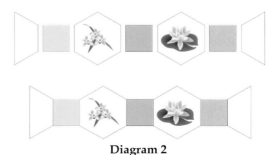

Diagram 2

3. *Triangle rows.* Referring to **Diagram 3**, stitch two Piece 3 triangles and two 4½" squares alternately together to make one unit. Repeat to make a total of 12 assorted color units. Sew three units together, and then attach another Piece 3 triangle to the right end to make one row. Repeat to make a total of four rows.

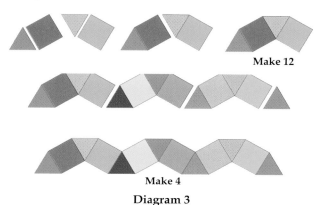

Make 12

Make 4

Diagram 3

Assembly

1. Following the **Quilt Layout Diagram**, stitch each of the top and bottom hexagon rows between two triangle rows. Pivot and flip the seam allowances as necessary to sew from marked point to marked point along each row.

2. Stitch the middle hexagon row between the top and bottom section, again sewing from marked point to marked point to complete the 34" x 37" quilt top.

3. Layer the quilt top right side up on top of the batting and the wrong side of the backing. Baste the layers together and quilt as desired. Trim the backing and batting even with the quilt top.

4. Bind using the 2½" white bias strips, pivoting as necessary to follow the outline of the quilt top. (See *General Quilting Directions*.)

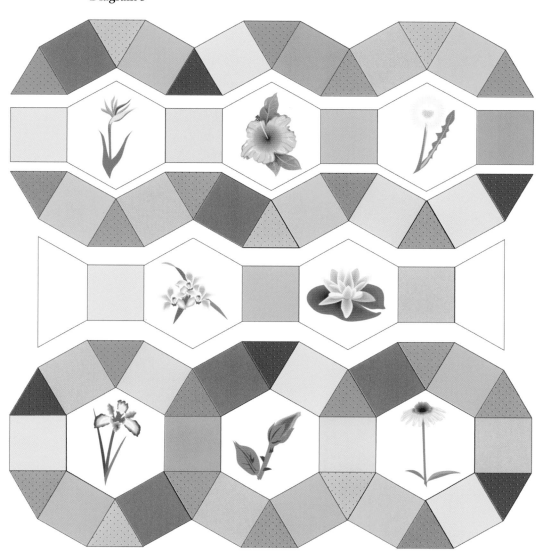

Diagram 4

Hand Mirror

Grandmother's Flower Garden Wall Hanging Companion Piece

Materials

- *Painter's Paradise* Old Fashion Hand Mirror
  www.paintersparadise.com)
- *Winsor & Newton Artists' Oil Colour:* Alizarin Crimson,
  French Ultramarine, Ivory Black, Olive Green, Prussian
  Blue, Terre Verte, Titanium White
- *DecoArt* Americana Acrylics: Bleached Sand, Silver
  Sage Green
- *Winsor & Newton* Regency Gold Golden Taklon #2, #4, #6,
  #8, and #10 synthetic short bright (Series 510), #0
  synthetic round (Series 520)
- *Loew-Cornell* La Cornielle Golden Taklon #10/0 Jackie
  Shaw liner (Series JS)
- *Blair* Satin Tole Spray varnish*
- *J.W. etc.* First-Step Wood Sealer
- *Masterson Art Products* Sta-Wet Palette
- *Winsor & Newton* Blending & Glazing Medium
- *Gane Brothers & Lane, Inc.* YES! Paste
- *Miscellaneous:* fine-line marker, 1" foam brush, gray
  graphite paper, sharp #2 lead pencil, odorless brush
  cleaner, palette knife, paper towels, sandpaper (200 grit,
  400 grit, and 600 grit), stylus, tape, tracing paper

Or varnish of choice (must be compatible with oil paint)

Preparation

1. Sand with 200-grit sandpaper, and wipe to remove dust. Seal with wood sealer. When dry, sand well and wipe.

2. Basecoat entire mirror with Bleached Sand and a 1" foam brush. Dry, and sand well. Paint the handle, edges, and back with Silver Sage Green. Dry.

3. Paint the hexagonal painting surface with Bleached Sand, and the handle, edges, and back with Silver Sage Green. Apply several coats, sanding between coats with 400-grit sandpaper, if needed. Dry thoroughly.

4. Trace design from Pattern Section, and transfer to surface with gray graphite and the stylus. Use the same design as for the quilt, replacing the leaves that cross over the stem on the bottom flower, and those to the right of it, with the leaves in the extra pattern provided.

Painting

Paint the design with oil colors, following the same technique as for the quilt, and substituting Blending & Glazing Medium for Transparent Medium. Use only a *very small* amount of medium, *stretching it* to cover, and working on several petals at a time.

Oil colors

Substitute oil colors for the fabric paints as follows:

Titanium White = White
French Ultramarine = Primary Blue
Prussian Blue + Titanium White = Mediterranean Blue
Alizarine Crimson + French Ultramarine + Titanium White = Lavender
Ivory Black = Lamp Black
Olive Green (add Titanium White for lighter green) = Avocado Green
Terre Verte + Titanium White (darker shading with Terre Verte + Ivory Black) = (Hauser Dark Green) + Avocado Green + White

Stamens and linework

Using the #10/0 liner, add a tiny teardrop-shaped Titanium White highlight to the black stamens. Thin Terre Verte + (Ivory Black) + (Titanium White) with odorless brush cleaner to the consistency of nail polish. Paint linework, including the narrow line that separates the Bleached Sand area from the handle.

Finishing

1. Varnish the painting following the manufacturer's directions. Allow to dry until cured—at least 48 hours.

2. When thoroughly cured, sand lightly with 600-grit sandpaper, being careful not to sand through to the painting. Spray with a final coat of varnish.

3. Attach mirror.

Garden Sampler Pillows

Jamie Mills-Price

Add a touch of whimsy to any room with birdhouses and airy, vine-enhanced designs. Paint them on fabric pillows, a simple box, or a wall plaque, and bring the outdoors inside!

Materials

- 2⅔ yards of light cream tonal fabric (for painted pillow tops; reserve remaining fabric for quilting instructions)
- *DecoArt* Americana Acrylics: Antique Mauve, Avocado, Burnt Umber, Cranberry Wine, Fawn, French Grey Blue, French Mauve, Honey Brown, Jade Green, Payne's Grey, Plantation Pine, Raw Sienna, Royal Purple, Soft Black, Summer Lilac, Warm White, Winter Blue, Yellow Ochre
- *Jo Sonja's* Sure Touch Golden Taklon #1 and #3 round (Series 1350), #2 detailer (Series 1355), #5/0 script liner (Series 1365), #2, # 8, and #10 flat (Series 1370), ½" and ¾" square wash (Series 1375); #2, #4, #6, and #8 Oval Dry Brush (ODB) (Series 2010)
- *DecoArt* Fabric Painting Medium
- *Miscellaneous:* gray graphite, paper towels, soft cloth, sturdy piece of stiff board (large), old toothbrush, pencil, plastic wrap, stylus, tape, tracing paper

Preparation

1. Wash, dry, and iron the fabric. Do not use fabric softener, dryer sheets, or spray starch.

2. Cut two 13" x 17" cream tonal pieces.

3. Cover a stiff board with smooth, taut plastic wrap. Tape fabric pieces onto prepared board.

4. Trace pattern from Pattern Section and lightly transfer the main pattern lines. Refer to the shading dots on the pattern for guidance while painting.

Painting

Note: Thin paint with a small amount of water to an inky consistency when instructions call for thinned paint.

Refer to the Worksheets on pages 29 and 30 as you paint.

Large Vine Wreath Pillow
Wreath

1. Load the #8 ODB with Fabric Painting Medium and cover the wreath, avoiding the pink flowers and leaves. (It is easiest to paint the wreath a section at a time, wet-on-wet, blending colors as you go.) Reload the #8 ODB with a mix of medium + Honey Brown, and paint the wreath with transparent color. Tip the dirty brush into Raw Sienna, and brush-blend into the shaded areas around flowers, leaves, and birdhouses. While wet, reload brush in medium and tip into Warm White. Brush highlights through the center of the wreath. Let dry.

2. Sideload the ¾" square wash with Raw Sienna, and softly shade around flowers, leaves, birdhouses, and along both sides of wreath. Deepen the floats next to the blue birdhouse and

around some flowers and leaves with a soft sideload of Burnt Umber.

3. Create a brush mix of thinned Raw Sienna + Warm White. Darken with a touch of Burnt Umber, if needed. Add medium to these inky puddles. Load the #2 detailer with Raw Sienna and begin stroking vine lines. Tip the brush into the lighter mix and highlight vines. Paint vine curlicues using same colors and a #5/0 script liner. Let dry.

Blue birdhouse

1. Load the #8 ODB with medium and cover the blue birdhouse. Do not wet the roof. While wet, load the dirty brush with Winter Blue and paint the house. Load the brush in a small amount of French Grey Blue, blending to shade. Add streaks on the house by tipping the brush on the chisel edge and pulling vertical strokes. Highlight with Warm White, using the same vertical strokes. Repeat the same technique and tint using Burnt Umber and Avocado. Let dry.

2. Sideload the ½" square wash with French Grey Blue + Payne's Grey, and float shading on the house. Deepen the shading with Payne's Grey. Using the same brush, float Warm White highlights, if needed.

Brown birdhouse

Use the same technique as for the blue birdhouse, but paint the house with Fawn, shade with medium + a small amount of Burnt Umber, highlight with Warm White, and tint with Jade Green. Dry. Float further shading with Burnt Umber, streak with Warm White highlights, and add tints of Antique Mauve.

Green birdhouse

Continue to use the same technique, but paint the house with Jade Green, shade with medium + a small amount of Avocado, highlight with Warm White, and tint with Fawn. Dry. Float further shading with Avocado, deepen with Plantation Pine, and streak with Warm White.

Birdhouse holes (all birdhouses)

Paint the hole with the #1 round brush and medium + Burnt Umber. Let dry. With the #8 flat, shade the inside bottom of the hole with Soft Black. The perch is a stylus dot of Soft Black. When dry, highlight with a dash of Warm White. Using the #8 flat, float a shadow of Burnt Umber below the perch.

Rooftops and grain lines (all birdhouses)

Load the #5/0 script liner with thinned Burnt Umber and paint the rooftops, using more pressure for bolder lines. With the same brush, pull fine grain lines over the houses and then lightly outline houses using less pressure for finer lines.

Pink flowers

1. Working the petals of one flower at a time, load the #2 ODB with medium and cover the petals. Reload the brush with medium and tip into French Mauve. Blend, and paint the petals. Tip the dirty brush into Antique Mauve, and blend. Pat-blend the color at the base of the petal and pull upward to streak.

2. Clean the brush and reload with medium. Tip into Warm White, and blend. Highlight outer edges of petals, blending downward as you go. Let dry. Sideload the #10 flat with Antique Mauve and shade petals. Deepen shading with small sideload of Cranberry Wine. Float soft tints of Avocado on some petals, if desired. Let dry. Using the #5/0 script liner, outline petals with thinned Antique Mauve and pull vein lines with thinned Cranberry Wine.

3. *Flower centers.* Load the #2 ODB with medium and cover the centers. Load the dirty brush with Yellow Ochre and paint the center. Tip the dirty brush into Warm White to highlight, and then into Raw Sienna. Let dry. Sideload the #10 flat with Raw Sienna and shade the center. Highlight with Warm White. Using the small end of the stylus, paint the Warm White pollen dots.

4. *Green leaves.* Working the leaves of one flower at a time, load the #2 ODB with medium and cover the leaves. Load the dirty brush with Jade Green and paint the leaves. Reload the #2 ODB with the medium and tip into Plantation Pine to shade. Highlight with Warm White. Let dry. Load the #5/0 script liner with thinned Plantation Pine and line the leaves. Line green vines with thinned Avocado.

Daisies

1. Load the #1 round with Warm White and stroke the daisy petals. Using the stylus, dot centers with Yellow Ochre and Raw Sienna.

2. With a mix of water + medium, thin puddles of Avocado, Plantation Pine, and Jade Green. Using the #3 round, stroke on the leaves, moving in and out of the colors, as desired.

Sampler Pillow
Bird panel

1. Load the #8 ODB with medium and cover the bird. Break the bird into sections, as it's easier to paint wet-on-wet, blending colors as you go. While the medium is still wet, reload the brush in the medium and tip into Winter Blue. Blend on the palette and paint the bird. Using the same brush, load with medium and sideload with French Grey Blue. Blend out over the shaded areas.

2. Reload with medium, tip in Warm White, and blend over the highlighted areas. Sideload the same brush with Warm White, tip the brush on the chisel edge, and tap over the body and wings to create the ruffled feather effects. Let dry.

3. Load the #2 ODB with medium + a touch of Yellow Ochre, and paint the beak. While wet, sideload the brush with a touch of Raw Sienna, fill the inside, and float the shading on the top of beak. Tip the brush in a touch of Warm White and highlight the beak. When dry, float a small amount of Raw Sienna + Burnt Umber inside the mouth.

Painted panel

4. Sideload the ½″ square wash with a brush mix of French Grey Blue + Payne's Grey, and float shading on the bird. Deepen shading in the darkest areas with floats of Payne's Grey. Sideload the ½″ square wash with Warm White, and float the highlight on the bird. Load the #3 round with medium + Warm White, and stroke the bright feathers on the wings and tail feathers. Let dry.

5. Sideload the ½″ square wash with Raw Sienna, and float tints on the wings and tail feathers. Sideload the ½″ square wash with Antique Mauve, and float a pink tint on the lower belly. Load a dry #8 ODB with a small amount of Antique Mauve, scrub on the palette, scrub on a paper towel, and softly scrub pink on the bird's cheeks. Line the eye using the #5/0 script liner and Burnt Umber.

6. *Bow tie and garland.* Line the bow tie using the #5/0 script liner with thinned Payne's Grey. Load the same brush with Burnt Umber, and stroke the wreath on the head. Add a few green vines with the liner and thinned Avocado. With the #3 round and thinned Avocado, stroke in small leaves. Load the #1 round with Antique Mauve, tip with Warm White, and stroke the flowers. Paint the centers with Yellow Ochre tipped in Raw Sienna.

7. *Twig.* Load the #2 ODB with medium + Fawn, and paint the twig. While wet, tip the brush in Burnt Umber to shade; tip in a touch of Warm White to highlight. When dry, line the twig using the #5/0 script liner and Burnt Umber. Line the feet and leg using the #5/0 script liner and thinned Burnt Umber. While wet, highlight the feet and leg with a touch of Fawn.

8. *Leaves.* Load the #2 ODB with medium + Jade Green, and paint the three leaves on the twig. While wet, load the brush in a small amount of Plantation Pine and blend to shade. Tip into Warm White and blend for highlight. Let dry. Using the ½″ square wash, tint the leaves with a soft sideload of Raw Sienna.

Twig heart panel

1. Stroke the twigs around the heart shape with Burnt Umber thinned with water + medium and the #5/0 script liner. Let dry. Load the #6 ODB with medium, and cover the inside of the heart and the twigs.

2. Sideload the ½″ square wash with Burnt Umber, and float over the twigs and in a couple of areas inside the heart. Sideload the ½″ square wash in Antique Mauve, and float a tint inside the heart; repeat with Avocado. Highlight with a float of Warm White in the upper left. When dry, add stylus dots of Warm White over the heart. Load the #2 flat with thinned Avocado, and stroke leaves on the twigs.

Pink flower panel

1. Load the #4 ODB with medium and cover the flower. Reload with medium, tip in French Mauve, and paint the petals. While wet, tip the dirty brush in a small amount of Antique Mauve and blend out for shading. Load with Warm White and blend out a highlight across the center of the petals. Let dry. Sideload the #10 flat with a brush mix of Antique Mauve + Cranberry Wine, and float the shading on the petals. Deepen with a touch of Cranberry Wine. Highlight the petal flip with a small sideload of Warm White. Line with Antique Mauve, and then add Cranberry Wine dots over the petals.

2. Load the #4 ODB with medium and cover the center. While wet, tip into Yellow Ochre and paint the center. Load the dirty brush with Raw Sienna and shade around the edges. Tip the brush into Warm White and highlight through center. Let dry.

3. Load the #4 ODB with medium and cover the leaves. Load the dirty brush with Jade Green and paint leaves. Load the dirty brush with Plantation Pine and shade. Highlight with Warm White. Let dry. Sideload the #10 flat with Plantation Pine, and float shading on leaves. Highlight further with Warm White. Add random Cranberry Wine tints. Line with Plantation Pine. Paint vines with thinned Avocado.

Wreath with birdhouses panel

1. Load the #6 ODB with medium and cover the round wreath. While wet, tip the dirty brush into Burnt Umber and blend out. Shade the beginning and end of the wreath. Reload the brush with medium and Warm White, and blend a highlight through the center. Let dry.

2. Sideload the ½″ square wash with Burnt Umber, and float both sides of wreath and deepen shading near birdhouse. Sideload the same brush with thinned Avocado, and float tints in a few areas of the wreath. Thin Burnt Umber with water + medium, and line the vinework over the wreath using a #2 detailer. Add fine curlicues using the #5/0 script liner.

3. *Pink birdhouse.* Load the #6 ODB with medium and cover the pink house. Do not cover the roof. While wet, load the dirty brush with French Mauve and cover the house. Load the dirty brush with Antique Mauve and shade the birdhouse. Reload with medium + Warm White, and highlight. Add streaks over the house. Paint the openings with the #3 round and Burnt Umber. Let dry.

4. Load the #5/0 script liner with thinned Warm White, and paint the plaid over the house. Sideload the ½″ square wash with Antique Mauve + Cranberry Wine, and float shading over the house. Deepen with floats of Cranberry Wine. Highlight with Warm White. If desired, sideload a small amount of Burnt Umber and float soft tints over the house. With Burnt Umber, float inside the holes and add the nail perches.

5. Load the #6 ODB with medium and cover the roof. While wet, load the dirty brush with Yellow Ochre and paint roof. While wet, load the dirty brush with Raw Sienna and shade roof. Reload with medium + Warm White, and highlight roof. Let dry.

6. Sideload the ½" square wash with Raw Sienna, and float shading on roof using dabby floats for texture. Deepen shading with Burnt Umber. Highlight with Warm White. Let dry. Load the ½" square wash with Avocado, and float soft tints over left side of roof.

7. Load the #5/0 script liner with Plantation Pine thinned with water + medium, and paint vines wrapping around roof. Pull brush through Jade Green, as needed, to highlight. Paint leaves with same colors using a #2 flat. Load a #1 round with Warm White, and stroke the daisy petals. The centers are Yellow Ochre tipped with Raw Sienna.

8. Load the ¾" square wash with medium, and brush the ground under house and wreath. Sideload the dirty brush with Avocado and float shading. Deepen shading with a soft sideload of Plantation Pine.

9. *Blue birdhouse.* Use the same technique as for the pink birdhouse, but paint the house Winter Blue, shade with a small amount of French Grey Blue, and highlight with Warm White. Paint the opening Burnt Umber. Dry. Paint the stripes Payne's Grey. Dry. Float shading of French Grey Blue + Payne's Grey. Deepen with Payne's Grey. Highlight with Warm White and tint over the right side with Avocado.

10. Continuing the same techniques, paint the roof Jade Green and shade with Plantation Pine. Highlight with medium + Warm White. Dry. Add dabby floats of Plantation Pine and highlight with Warm White. Dry. Float soft tints of Burnt Umber over right side of roof. Dot and line the tip of the rooftop with Plantation Pine.

Tulips

1. *Yellow tulips.* Load the #2 ODB with medium and cover the petals. Load the dirty brush with Yellow Ochre and paint yellow tulip petals. Load the dirty brush with small amount of Raw Sienna, and shade. Reload with medium, tip into Warm White, and add streaky highlights through the petals. Let dry. Using the #10 flat and a small sideload of Raw Sienna, deepen shading as needed. Float bright highlights with a sideload of Warm White. Sideload the brush with a small amount of Cranberry Wine, and tint lower sides of petals.

2. *Pink tulips.* Use the same technique as for the yellow tulips, but paint petals with French Mauve, shade with Antique Mauve, and highlight with Warm White. Dry. Further shade with Antique Mauve + Cranberry Wine. Float bright highlights of Warm White. Tint with Avocado.

3. *Purple tulip.* Continue to use same technique, using Summer Lilac for the petals. Shade with Royal Purple and highlight with Warm White.

Deepen the shading with more Royal Purple, and float bright highlights with Warm White. Tint with Raw Sienna.

4. *Tulip leaves and stems.* Load the #2 ODB with medium and cover leaf fronds and stems. Load the dirty brush with Jade Green, and paint all leaves and stems. Sideload the dirty brush with a small amount of Plantation Pine, and shade. Reload with medium, tip into Warm White, and paint streaky highlights. Refine stems using the #3 round, as needed. Let dry.

Deepen shading with a #10 flat and a small sideload of Plantation Pine. Highlight stems with a #3 round and Warm White. Sideload the brush with a small amount of Cranberry Wine, and tint lower sides of leaves.

5. *Vine separations.* Load the #2 detailer with Burnt Umber thinned with water + medium. Stroke the vines. Add fine curlicues of Burnt Umber with the #5/0 script liner.

6. *Shadows.* Load a dry #8 ODB with a small amount of Avocado, scrub the brush on the palette, then remove nearly all paint on a paper towel. Scrub softly under the houses and wreath. Scrub nearly all color out of the brush (do not wash), and load with a small amount of Burnt Umber; repeat process, scrubbing softly under elements for a shadowy effect.

Finishing

1. If desired, spatter the fabric with thinned Burnt Umber and an old toothbrush. Let dry.

2. Heat-set the design by placing a cloth over the dry painted design. Never iron directly on the paint. Using a temperature appropriate for the fabric, iron one section at a time for 20 to 30 seconds. Heat-set reverse side in same manner.

Painted panel

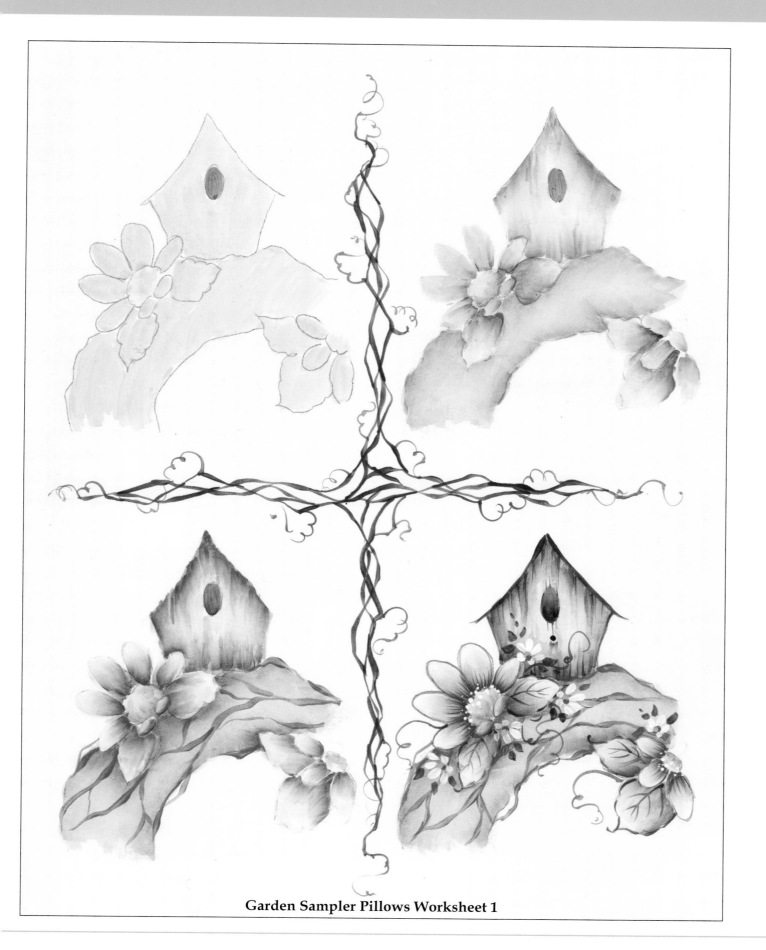

Garden Sampler Pillows Worksheet 1

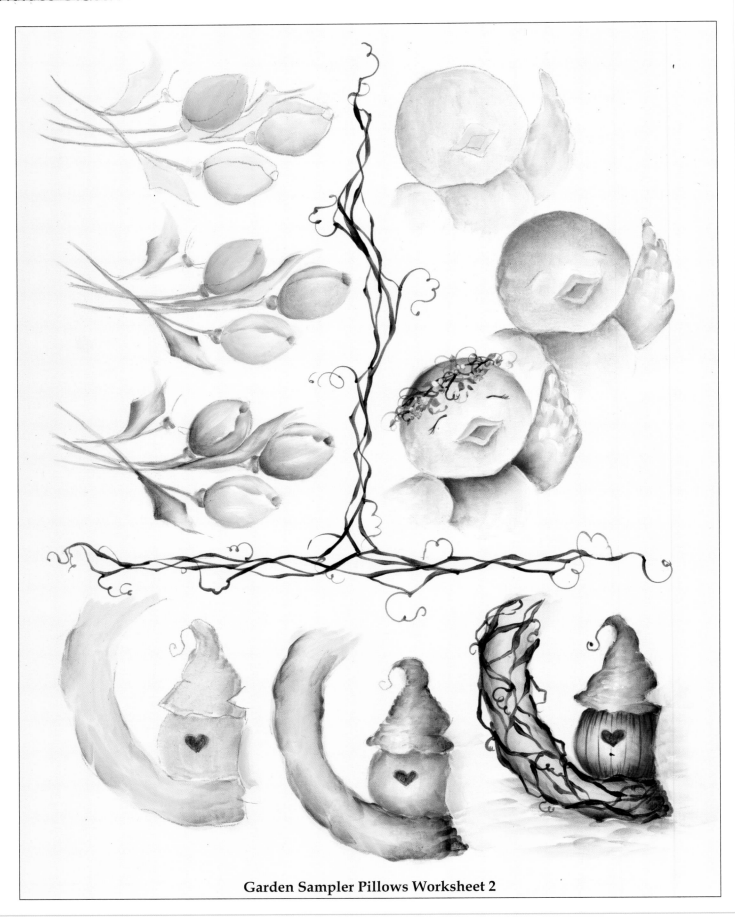

Garden Sampler Pillows Worksheet 2

Quilting
Pillows pieced and quilted
by Cindy Gensamer

Skill level: Beginner/Intermediate
Finished pillow size: 20″ x 24½″

Materials

Note: Yardage is based on 42″ wide useable fabric. Material list includes the fabric and supplies for two pillows.
- Two painted panels trimmed to 11½″ x 16″
- ¼ yard light blue tonal fabric
- ⅝ yard muslin fabric
- ⅞ yard cream print fabric (includes border and backing)
- Reserved light cream tonal fabric (same fabric as the painted panels, for ruffle)
- Two 19″ x 24″ pieces of batting
- Thread in colors to match fabrics
- Fiberfill stuffing
- Basic sewing and rotary cutting supplies

Cutting

From the light blue tonal, cut:
Three 1″ x 42″ strips; recut into four 1″ x 11½″ strips and four 1″ x 16″ strips

From the muslin, cut:
One 17″ x 42″ strip; recut into two 17″ x 21″ pieces

From the cream print, cut:
Four 1¾″ x 42″ strips; recut into four 1¾″ x 16″ strips and four 1¾″ x 13½″ strips (for borders)
One 15″ x 42″ strip; recut into two 15″ x 19½″ pieces (for backing)

From the light cream tonal, cut:
Eight 8″ x 42″ strips (for ruffle)

Assembly

Note: Use a ¼″ seam allowance throughout, unless otherwise indicated. Sew all pieces with right sides together and raw edges even, using matching thread. Refer to the pillow photo on page 24 for steps 1 through 5.

1. *Dimensional border.* Fold each 1″ wide light blue tonal strip in half lengthwise wrong sides together and press. Lay one 16″ folded strip on each long side of one 11½″ x 16″ painted panel, lining up the raw edges. Baste in place using a ⅛″ seam allowance. Attach the 11½″ folded strips to the short sides of the painted panel in the same manner. (This folded border will remain on top of the painted panel.)

2. *Border.* Sew the 1½″ x 16″ cream print strips to the long sides of the painted panel. Press seams toward the border strips, leaving the blue dimensional border on top of the painted panel. Stitch the 13½″ long strips to the remaining sides in the same manner.

3. Lay the pillow top right side up on top of the batting and one 19″ x 42″ piece of muslin. Baste in place and quilt as desired. (*Note:* The quilting in the featured pillows outlined the painted motifs.) Trim the batting and muslin even with the pillow top.

4. *Ruffle.* Sew four 8″ x 42″ light cream tonal strips short ends together to make one long strip. Press under ½″ along one short end, then press the strip lengthwise in half with the wrong sides together. Double thread a needle, and starting ½″ in from the folded end, use a long basting stitch to sew a scant ¼″ away from the raw edges along the length of the fabric. Pull the threads, gathering the fabric evenly until it measures 68″ long, and tie a knot.

Leaving a 3″ tail and starting with the folded end, align the raw edges of the ruffle with the pillow top, right side up. Baste the ruffle to the quilt top using a ¼″ seam allowance and easing at each corner. Stop sewing 3″ away from the beginning stitches. Place the end of the ruffle inside the folded end (beginning), so that the folded end is on the outside. Trim away excess from the tucked, unfolded end to ¼″. Align the raw edges and finish basting the ruffle to the pillow top.

5. Leaving the ruffle on top of the pillow top, place the 15″ x 19½″ cream print piece right sides together with the pillow top, aligning the raw edges. Stitch using a ½″ seam allowance around the perimeter, pivoting at each corner. Leave a small opening on one side to insert the stuffing. Trim the seam allowances at each corner, turn right side out, and stuff using the fiberfill. Turn in the seam allowance ½″ and hand-stitch the opening closed.

6. Repeat steps 1 through 5 with the other painted panel.

Garden Sampler Boxes

Garden Sampler Pillows Companion Piece

Materials

- *Valhalla Designs* Large Bombay Box (rectangular) #LSMB-26 (11"x 9"x 3") and Large Round Shallow Box, #LRSH-145 (10"x 2") (www.valhalladesigns.com)
- *DecoArt* Americana Acrylics: Antique Mauve, Avocado, Burnt Umber, Cranberry Wine, Fawn, French Grey Blue, French Mauve, Honey Brown, Jade Green, Light Buttermilk, Mississippi Mud, Payne's Grey, Plantation Pine, Raw Sienna, Soft Black, Warm White, Winter Blue, Yellow Ochre
- *Jo Sonja's* Sure Touch Golden Taklon #1 and #3 round (Series 1350), #2 detailer (Series 1355), #5/0 script liner (Series 1365), #2, #4, # 8, #10 flat (Series 1370), ½" and ¾" square wash (Series 1375); #2, #4, #6, and #8 Oval Dry Brush (ODB) (Series 2010)
- *DecoArt* Multi-Purpose Sealer; DuraClear Matte Varnish
- *DUCK Brand* Wall Repair Fabric (self-adhesive fiberglass)
- *Miscellaneous:* eraser, gray graphite, old toothbrush, paper towels, plastic wrap, sandpaper, stylus, tape, tracing paper

Preparation

1. Sand and seal with sealer + Light Buttermilk. Sand again.

2. Basecoat with straight Light Buttermilk. Let dry. Sand again lightly, and wipe.

3. Trace pattern from Pattern Section and transfer main pattern lines, omitting details.

Bottom of Heart Wreath Box

1. Stain the bottom of the box with sealer + thinned Honey Brown. Wipe off excess with a paper towel. Let dry, and sand lightly.

2. Adhere Wall Repair Fabric to the box bottom. Stipple Light Buttermilk through the fabric. When dry, remove fabric from the box to reveal a checkered effect. Float the edges with Raw Sienna; deepen with Burnt Umber.

Painting

Note: Thin the paint with water to an inky consistency when thinned paint is needed.

Heart Wreath Bombay Box

1. *Lid.* Paint the checks on the lid with a #10 flat and thinned Honey Brown.

2. Follow instructions for the heart wreath with birdhouses pillow; however, instead of using Fabric Painting Medium, use basic floating techniques.

3. Float around the elements and on the lid top with Mississippi Mud. Float soft random tints on the lid with colors from the palette.

4. *Bottom of box.* Paint small, scattered daisies similar to the small white flowers on the wreath. Float around the centers with a sideload of Antique Mauve.

Birdhouses on Round Wreath Box

1. *Lid.* Follow the instructions for the round

wreath with birdhouses pillow; however, use basic floating techniques without Fabric Painting Medium.

2. Float around the elements and on the lid top with Mississippi Mud. Float soft random tints on the lid with colors from the palette.

3. Paint small Warm White checks along the top using the #4 flat.

4. *Flowers.* The flowers on the wreath are similar to the ones on the yellow roof; add a float around the centers with a soft sideload of Antique Mauve.

Load the #1 round with French Grey Blue, tip in Warm White, and stroke small blue flowers onto the yellow roof and wreath. Paint the centers Yellow Ochre. Stroke the small leaves using the #1 round and thinned Plantation Pine. Double-load the #8 flat with Jade Green and Plantation Pine, and paint the large leaves on the wreath. Line the little connecting vines with Burnt Umber. Using the #5/0 script liner and thinned Plantation Pine and Jade Green, add grass under the birdhouse and wreath, moving in and out of the colors.

5. Using the ¾" square wash and thinned Plantation Pine, apply the checks on the edge of the lid. Float the top of the checks with Plantation Pine.

6. Load the #1 round with Antique Mauve, tip in Warm White, and stroke the small flower clusters on the lid. Load the #1 round with thinned Plantation Pine and stroke the little leaves.

Finishing

Erase any remaining graphite lines. Following the manufacturer's instructions, varnish with matte varnish.

Celebrate the Seasons Wall Hanging

Jo Sonja Jansen

A sampler of folk art birds celebrates the seasons and reminds us of cherished moments during the year.

Materials
- Four 9½" x 12" pieces of cotton fabric (light backgrounds)
- *Chroma, Inc.* Jo Sonja's Artists' Colours: Brilliant Green, Carbon Black, Gold Oxide, Napthol Crimson, Orange, Purple Madder, Red Violet, Sapphire, Titanium White, Ultramarine Blue, Yellow Orange
- *Jo Sonja's* Sure Touch Artist's Brushes #2, #6, and #8 oval dry brush (Series 2010) for basic painting; #2 short liner (Series 1360) for fine details
- *Chroma, Inc.* Jo Sonja's Textile Medium
- *Miscellaneous:* freezer wrap (cut to size of background fabric), fine-tip permanent marker, light box*, paper towels, #2HB pencil, 9x12 sheet of coarse sandpaper, scissors, tape, tracing paper, small containers for medium
  *optional

Preparation
1. Wash, dry, and iron fabric pieces. Do not use fabric softener, dryer sheets, or spray starch. Cut fabric pieces.

2. Trace design from Pattern Section and transfer to the shiny side of the freezer wrap with the permanent marker.

3. Lay fabric piece right side up on top of freezer wrap. Using the cotton setting on the iron, press the fabric onto the freezer wrap; this holds the fabric firmly in place while transferring the design. Tape the fabric to a window, or over a light box, and transfer the design using the pencil.

4. Remove fabric from freezer wrap and lay fabric, right side up, on a piece of sandpaper to hold the fabric in place while painting.

Techniques
- Pour about one tablespoon each of Textile Medium and water into a small container. Mix well, and cover when not in use. If medium dries out, make a fresh mix. Dip the brush in medium and place a dot on the palette. Load the brush with an equal amount of the desired color and mix into the medium. Blot the brush on a paper towel, and gently paint the fabric using a light brushing motion. Control the amount of paint going onto the fabric by the amount of the pressure on the brush. Always blot the brush before painting.
- Paint shadows using the same techniques and a sideloaded brush.
- Keep color application gentle and delicate. It's best that the paint does not penetrate through to the back side of the fabric.

Painting
Main elements

Note: Using the appropriate-sized oval dry brush, gently brush the following colors into the fabric. Refer to the photos for placement. Remember to load each color using the medium mix explained in Techniques above.

Allow the background fabric to show through for highlights. It may be necessary to add a tiny touch of Titanium White here and there to further brighten.

Refer to the Worksheets on pages 36-38 as you paint.

1. Use Napthol Crimson to basecoat the hearts, winter bird's wings, stripes on the flag, and red areas on all squares. Shade with Red Violet, adding touches of Purple Madder here and there. If more highlights are needed, add a touch of Titanium White.

2. Base the pumpkin, body of the spring bird, large heart details, and other orange areas with Orange. Shade with Gold Oxide, with touches of Purple Madder to vary. Add a small blush of Yellow Orange or a touch of Titanium White for further highlights, as desired.

3. Base the pears and other yellow areas with Yellow Orange. Shade with Gold Oxide. If more highlights are needed, add a touch of Titanium White.

4. Base the green areas with Brilliant Green. Shade with Brilliant Green + a touch of Ultramarine Blue or Carbon Black. Highlight with Yellow Orange, adding a touch of Titanium White where desired. Deepen the shading at the base of the leaves and on the pumpkin stem with an Olive Green mixture of Brilliant Green + a touch of Napthol Crimson.

5. Basecoat the flowers, summer bird, blue field on the flag, and other blue areas with Sapphire. Shade with Sapphire + a touch of Ultramarine Blue or Carbon Black. Further brighten some highlights with a touch of Titanium White.

6. Paint the blackbirds and black areas with Sapphire. Shade with Carbon Black. To further brighten highlights, add a touch of Titanium White where desired.

7. Use the fabric as the basecoat for all unpainted white areas. Shade with a touch of Sapphire. Add a touch of Titanium White to highlight.

8. Referring to the photo for placement, accent with touches of purple brush mixes of Red Violet + Ultramarine Blue.

Painted panel

Details

Note: Paint the dabby spots with the #2 oval dry brush.

1. *Spring panel.* Using the #2 short liner, paint comma stroke leaves with Brilliant Green. Return and casually stroke a touch of Gold Oxide here and there. Dab dots of Gold Oxide with the #2 oval dry brush. Casually sprinkle in some Yellow Orange dots.

Celebrate the Seasons Spring Worksheet

Painted panel

2. *Summer panel.* Shade the Gold Oxide flagpole, bird legs, and cord with dabs of Purple Madder. Using the #2 oval dry brush, base the stars with dabs of Titanium White. Touch here and there with the liner, adding points to the stars. Add a casual hint of Yellow Orange to the bird's wing. Add a line of Titanium White dots along the side of the wing. On the bird's breast, paint a few dabs of Napthol Crimson and add a soft blush on the cheek. Paint soft swirls of color for the fireworks using the colors from the palette. Dab very soft spots in a progression of colors around the swirls.

Celebrate the Seasons Summer Worksheet

Painted panel

3. *Autumn panel.* Reinforce the orange progression on pumpkin. Deepen the shadows of the pumpkin with a touch of Napthol Crimson; add Red Violet to the deepest shadows. Begin the birds and pumpkin face details with Sapphire. Shade with Carbon Black. Add dabs of Carbon Black on the bird's breast. Blush the cheek and paint the red on the wings with Napthol Crimson. Begin the oak leaves with Yellow Orange, and then shade with Brilliant Green, adding touches of Gold Oxide.

Celebrate the Seasons Autumn Worksheet

Painted panel

4. *Winter panel.* Accent the pears with yellow progressions, blush Orange, or Napthol Crimson or Brilliant Green, as desired. Very lightly touch the bird's tummy with Yellow Orange. Shade with Sapphire, adding touches of Carbon Black. Dab the berries with dots of Napthol Crimson, and shade with a touch of Purple Madder. Dab extra dots with Orange, and then a few with Yellow Orange.

Finishing

1. Using the #2 short liner, paint the lettering, strokes, and linework details with either Purple Madder or Carbon Black, or a mix of the two colors.

2. When the panels are dry, heat-set using the iron on the cotton setting. Place a piece of clean tracing paper over the top of the panel, and iron for about 15 seconds. Remove tracing paper and iron again. Flip the fabric over and iron the back.

Celebrate the Seasons Winter Worksheet

Quilting
Quilt designed, pieced, and quilted
by *Cindy Gensamer*

Skill level: Beginner
Finished panel size: 8½" x 18½"
Number of panels: 4
Finished quilt size: 23" x 46"

Materials

Note: Yardage is based on 42" wide useable fabric.
- Four painted blocks trimmed to 9" x 11½"
- One fat eighth (9" x 22") each of 11 assorted light, medium, and dark value small scale prints
- 1 yard dark brown print (includes binding)
- 30" x 54" piece of backing fabric
- 30" x 54" piece of batting
- Thread in colors to match fabrics
- Basic sewing and rotary cutting supplies

Cutting

From each of the assorted small scale prints:
Two 2" x 9" pieces

From the dark brown print:
One 2" x 42" strip; recut into four 2" x 9" pieces
Three 3" x 42" strips; recut into five 3" x 19" strips (for sashing)
Three 3" x 42" strips (for borders)
Four 2½" x 42" strips (for binding)

Directions

Note: Use a ¼" seam allowance throughout. Sew all pieces with right sides together and raw edges even, using matching thread. Press all seams toward the darker fabric.

1. Following **Diagram 1** and using 2" x 9" pieces, sew four assorted light to medium color pieces lengthwise together to make one 6½" x 9" pieced unit. Repeat to make a second unit. Using the medium to dark color pieces, make a total of two darker pieced units. (*Note:* Some pieces will be left over.)

Diagram 1

2. Stitch a 2" x 9" dark brown piece to the right side of each of the spring and autumn panels, and the left side of the summer and winter panels as shown in **Diagram 2**. Stitch the lighter pieced sections to the spring and summer panels, and the darker pieced sections to the autumn and winter panels to complete four 9" x 19" sections.

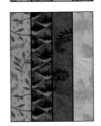

Diagram 2

Assembly

1. Referring to the **Quilt Layout Diagram** and noting placement of each season, sew a 3" x 19" dark brown strip alternately together with the four sections.

2. Cut one 3" x 42" dark brown strip in half to equal two 3" x 21" lengths. Stitch each half strip to a remaining dark brown strip. Sew these long strips to the sides of the quilt top. Press and trim the excess.

3. Layer the quilt top right side up on top of the batting and the wrong side of the backing. Baste the layers together and quilt as desired. Trim the batting and the backing even with the quilt top.

4. Bind using four 2½" x 42" dark brown strips. (See *General Quilting Directions*.)

Exploded View of Quilt Layout Diagran

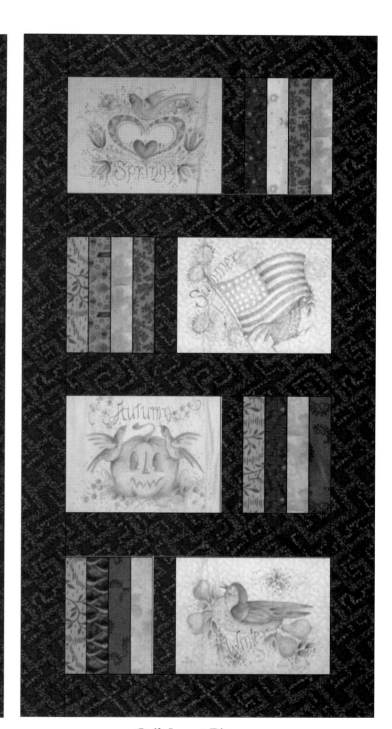

Quilt Layout Diagran

Old Tin Coffeepot

Celebrate the Seasons Wall Hanging Companion Piece

Materials

- Coffeepot of choice*
- *Chroma, Inc.* Jo Sonja's Artists' Colours: Brilliant Green, Carbon Black, Gold Oxide, Napthol Crimson, Orange, Purple Madder, Red Violet, Sapphire, Titanium White, Ultramarine Blue, Yellow Orange
- *Chroma, Inc.* Jo Sonja's Background Colours: Cashmere, Island Sand
- *Jo Sonja's* Sure Touch Artist's Brushes #4 and #6 flat (Series 1370) or #4 and #6 filbert (Series 1385), #3 or #4 round (Series 1350), #2 short liner (Series 1360); #2, #6, and #8 oval dry brush (Series 2010) (optional)
- *Chroma, Inc.* Jo Sonja's All Purpose Sealer, Jo Sonja's Matte Varnish (polyurethane)
- *Miscellaneous:* coarse sandpaper or emery cloth, #2HB pencil, soft cloth, stylus, tracing paper, transfer paper

Shown is an antique tin coffeepot. Resize or rearrange designs to fit your piece.

Preparation

1. Thoroughly clean the piece. Sand and remove dust.

2. Apply one or two coats of All Purpose Sealer. Dry well.

3. Basecoat the entire surface with Cashmere or Island Sand.

4. Base details with washes of color. Wash blue stripes with Sapphire; shade with Sapphire + Ultramarine Blue or Carbon Black. Add stars with Titanium White. Wash handle and spout with Yellow Orange; shade with Gold Oxide. Wash knob and striped bands with Orange; shade with Gold Oxide + a touch of Purple Madder.

5. Trace pattern from Pattern Section and transfer to surface.

Painting

1. The instructions for painting the coffeepot follow the same progression as the fabric piece. Do not use the Textile Medium mix.

2. Using an appropriate-sized brush and basic strokes, basecoat each area. Refer to the photo for placement. Shade and highlight with strokes, or drybrush using the oval dry brushes from the fabric painting.

Finishing

When dry, finish with several coats of matte varnish. Allow adequate drying time between each application.

A Gala of Fruit Wall Hanging

Mary Wiseman

This gala of fruit brings the realistic still life design to fabric, creating a wall hanging that showcases two creative art forms.

Materials
- ½ yard white tone-on-tone fabric
- *DecoArt* Americana SoSoft Fabric Acrylics: Antique Gold, Avocado Green, Brown, Buttermilk, Burnt Sienna, Cadmium Yellow, Canary Yellow, Crimson, Indian Turquoise, Lamp Black, Navy Blue, White, Wine, Yellow Green
- *Loew-Cornell* White Nylon ⅛", ¼", ⅜", and ½" angular flat (Series 793), #6/0 liner (Series 801), #2 round (Series 795)
- *DecoArt* Americana Transparent Medium
- *Miscellaneous:* freezer paper (waxed), heavy foam core board or cardboard, masking tape, stylus, tracing paper, transfer paper, waxed-paper palette, wet palette or small paint cups for mixes

Preparation

1. Wash and dry the fabric before painting. Do not use any fabric softener. From the white tone-on-tone, cut one each of the following pieces: 12" x 13" (for grapes), 9" x 6½" (for pears), 9½" x 5" (for plums), 9½" x 8½" (for apples), and 6½" x 5" (for peach).

2. Cut a piece of freezer paper to the size of your fabric. Place the freezer paper shiny side against the wrong side of the fabric, and using a dry, hot iron, press the right side of the fabric to secure the paper to the fabric. Tape the fabric square to the foam core board or to the heavy cardboard.

3. Trace the pattern from Pattern Section and transfer design to fabric squares with the stylus.

Techniques

- *Stage 1 painting:* Basecoat with the color listed. Dress the brush with Transparent Medium and cover the desired area. Apply the color with a sideload or a fully loaded brush without any water. Use more paint on the brush than when painting with other acrylic paints.
- *Stage 2 painting:* Apply a second basecoat over the dry first coat. While wet, apply the shade color using a pat-pull method, working the color into the fabric. Repeat, using the light value, and blend into the wet basecoat. The base color is the transition between the light and the dark value. Work most colors wet-on-wet.
- *Stage 3 painting:* For stronger lights, drybrush over dry paint. Achieve darker values using a sideload of color. Thin colors for washes or floats with water or medium.
- *Stage 4 painting:* Complete all details with a #2 round or liner, depending on area.

Painting

Note: Refer to the Worksheet on page 47 for step-by-step illustrations of plums and berries.

The plus sign (+) between colors indicates a mix made of these colors.

Plums, leaves, and berries

1. Basecoat plums with a mix of Wine + Indian Turquoise (Base mix). Shade with Wine + a touch of Navy Blue. Add a Base mix + Buttermilk highlight. Deepen shading with Wine + Lamp Black + a touch of Navy Blue. Highlight with White. Add reflected light with a light gray-blue mix of White + a touch of Navy.

2. Base the leaves with Canary Yellow + a touch of Avocado Green (Base mix). Shade with Avocado Green + Antique Gold. Deepen shading with Avocado Green + Brown. Highlight with Base mix + Buttermilk. Paint vein lines with Crimson + Brown. Add accents with Wine or a purple mix of Wine + Navy Blue.

3. Paint berries with Buttermilk + a touch of Yellow Green. Highlight with Buttermilk. Shade with a mix of the base + a touch of Crimson.

4. Base the stems and branches with a mix of Avocado Green + Brown. Highlight stems and branches with Buttermilk.

Peach and blueberries

1. Basecoat the peach with Canary Yellow. Shade with Cadmium Yellow + Antique Gold + a touch of Crimson. Deepen shading with Wine. Highlight with White + Canary Yellow. Add Indian Turquoise accents.

2. Base leaves with Canary Yellow + Antique Gold + Lamp Black. Shade with Antique Gold + a touch of Lamp Black. Highlight with Canary Yellow. Add Crimson tints. Paint veins with Canary Yellow + White.

3. Base blueberries with Navy Blue + Indian Turquoise (Base mix). Shade with Navy Blue. Deepen shading with Navy Blue + a touch of Lamp Black. Highlight with White + Base mix. Add final highlight with White. Paint the blossom end with Lamp Black.

4. Paint the peach stem with Brown. Highlight with Brown + Buttermilk.

Pears

1. Paint the center pear with Cadmium Yellow + Buttermilk + a touch of Yellow Green. Shade with Cadmium Yellow + Antique Gold. Highlight with Canary Yellow. Add accents with Yellow Green and Crimson. Add final highlight with White.

2. Base the left pear with Antique Gold + Yellow Green. Shade first with Yellow Green, then with Crimson. Highlight with Cadmium Yellow + Canary Yellow. Add the final highlight with White.

3. Base the right pear with Antique Gold. Shade with Burnt Sienna. Highlight with Cadmium Yellow + Buttermilk. Accent the front lower area with Yellow Green.

4. Create pear stems with Brown + a touch of Lamp Black. Highlight with White.

5. Load the round brush with Brown thinned with medium. Lightly spatter the pears to create a blemished appearance.

Apples, blackberries, and leaves

1. Base apples with Antique Gold + Canary Yellow + Yellow Green. Shade with Antique Gold + Yellow Green. Deepen shading with Antique Gold + Yellow Green + Brown. Add the highlight with Canary Yellow. Reinforce with

Canary Yellow + White, then with straight White. Accent with Crimson + Brown. Add reflected light with Canary Yellow + a touch of Yellow Green + a touch of Indian Turquoise.

2. Thin Brown + a touch of Lamp Black with water or medium, and paint the apple stem and blossom end. Pull out small hairs at the blossom end. Load the dirty brush with Buttermilk. Place highlights and, if desired, drag a little bit of Buttermilk over the wet stem.

3. Base leaves with Canary Yellow + a touch of Avocado Green (Base mix). Shade with Avocado Green + Antique Gold. Deepen shading with Avocado Green + Brown. Highlight with Base mix + Buttermilk. Create vein lines with Crimson + Brown. Accent with Wine or a purple mix of Wine + Navy Blue.

4. Base blackberries with Indian Turquoise + Wine (Base mix). Shade with Wine + a touch of Navy Blue; adding more Navy Blue makes the color more purple. Highlight with Base mix + White. Thin Buttermilk with water to an inky consistency, and paint the blackberry seed cells. Using the liner, start in the center and paint a full row of complete circles. Continue lining the cells on each side of the full circles in rows of half circles.

Using the ⅛" angular flat, float a light value on each of the cells using Buttermilk + Base mix (1:1). Float the light value on either the left or right side of each cell; the center circles have light areas on both sides. Create a red-violet mix of Wine + Navy Blue + a touch of Lamp Black. Using washes and floats of this mix, shade over the berry seed cells and strengthen the shade areas. Repeat for darker berries. Highlight each seed with White + Buttermilk. Pull small hairs out of the berries using Lamp Black. Paint the caps using the leaf colors.

Grapes and leaves

1. Base green leaves with Canary Yellow. Shade with Yellow Green + Antique Gold. Deepen dark areas with Avocado Green + Antique Gold. Highlight with Canary Yellow + White. Using the liner, paint the vein

lines with Crimson + Brown or Avocado Green + Brown. Accent with Wine, Wine + Crimson, or Antique Gold.

2. Paint yellow leaves with Canary Yellow. Shade with Antique Gold. Deepen the shading with Antique Gold + Brown or Antique Gold + Wine. Highlight with Canary Yellow + White. Paint vein lines with Avocado Green + Brown. Paint accents with Wine, Wine + Crimson, or Antique Gold.

3. Base grapes with Wine + Canary Yellow + a touch of White (Base mix). Shade with Wine + Canary Yellow. Add more White to the Base mix and highlight each grape. Deepen the shading first with Wine + Crimson, then with Wine or

Wine + a touch of Lamp Black in the darkest areas. Highlight each grape with White. Add reflected light with White + a touch of Navy Blue. Reinforce the final highlight with straight White. Wash Antique Gold accents over the light area of a few grapes.

4. Base branches with a wash of Brown + Antique Gold. While wet, shade the branch using straight Brown, patting randomly onto the branch area.

Finishing

Heat-setting is not required. Allow 72 hours before washing.

Gala of Fruit Worksheet

Quilting
Quilt designed, pieced, and quilted
by Cindy Gensamer

Skill level: Beginner/Intermediate
Finished wall hanging size: 28½" x 30½"

Materials

Note: Yardage is based on 42" wide useable fabric.
- One painted grape panel trimmed to 11½" x 12½"
- One painted apple panel trimmed to 9" x 8"
- One painted plum panel trimmed to 9" x 4½"
- One painted pear panel trimmed to 8½" x 6"
- One painted peach panel trimmed to 6" x 4½"
- ⅛ yard each of twelve different batik fabrics in colors to match the fruit motifs
- ⅜ yard cream tonal fabric
- ¾ yard tan tonal fabric (includes binding)
- 34" x 37" piece of backing fabric
- 34" x 37" piece of batting
- Thread in colors to match fabrics
- Basic sewing and rotary cutting supplies

Cutting

From each of the twelve different batiks, cut:
One 1½" x 42" strip; recut each strip into four 1½" x 2½" pieces

From the cream tonal, cut:
Five 1½" x 42" strips; recut into two each of the following lengths: 14½", 11½", 10", 6", 8½", 8", and four lengths each 6½" and 9" (for painted panel frames)

From the tan, cut:
One 3½" x 42" strip; recut into one each of the following lengths: 13½", 10", and 8"
Five 2½" x 42" strips; recut into two 17" lengths, two 15" lengths, and one 10½" length
One 2" x 42" strip; recut into one 2" x 11" piece and one 2" x 8" piece
Two 1½" x 42" strips; recut into one each of the following lengths: 26", 12", and 11"

Directions

Note: Use a ¼" seam allowance throughout. Sew all pieces with right sides together and raw edges even, using matching thread. In steps 1 through 5, press all seams away from the painted panels after adding each strip.

1. *Grape section.* Following **Diagram 1** and using 1½" wide cream tonal pieces, sew one 11½" length to the top of the grape panel and another to the bottom. Stitch the 14½" lengths to the sides.

Diagram 1

2. *Pear section.* Referring to **Diagram 2** and using 1½" wide cream tonal pieces, sew one 8½" length to the top of the pear panel and another to the bottom. Stitch an 8" length to each side. Using the tan tonal pieces, sew a 2½" x 10½" piece to the bottom of the panel unit, stitch a 3½" x 10" piece to the right side, and then a 3½" x 13½" piece to the top.

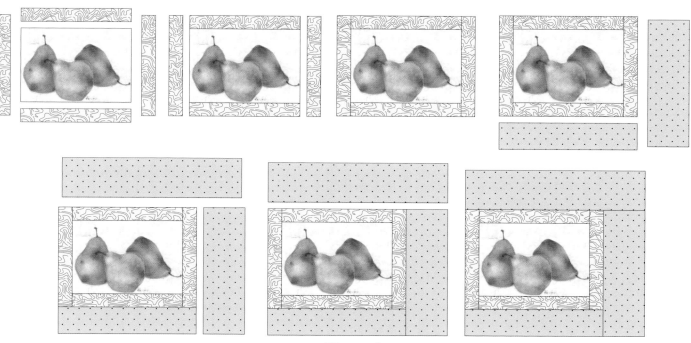

Diagram 2

3. *Peach section.* Again using 1½" wide cream tonal pieces, sew a 6" length to the top of the peach panel and another to the bottom. Stitch the 6½" lengths to the sides as shown in **Diagram 3**. Sew the 2" x 8" tan piece to the bottom of the panel unit, then stitch the 3½" x 8" tan piece to the left side.

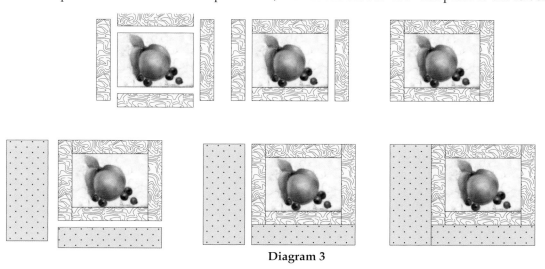

Diagram 3

4. *Apple section.* Following **Diagram 4** and using 1½" wide cream tonal pieces, sew a 9" length to the top of the apple panel and another to the bottom. Stitch a 10" length to each side.

Diagram 4

5. *Plum section.* Sew the remaining 9" cream tonal lengths to the top and bottom of the plum panel and the 6½" lengths to the sides as shown in **Diagram 5**. Stitch a 2" x 11" tan piece to the top and a 1½" x 11" tan piece to the bottom.

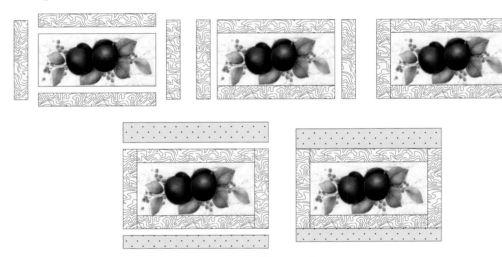

Diagram 5

Assembly

Note: Refer to the **Quilt Layout Diagram** for steps 1 and 2.

1. Sew the pear section to the bottom of the grape section. Next, stitch the apple section between the peach and plum sections, then sew the 1½" x 26" tan strip to the left side, and the 1½" x 12" tan piece to the top. Stitch the apple/peach/plum section to the grape/pear section to complete the 25" x 27" quilt center.

2. *Border.* Noting color placement, sew twelve 1½" x 2½" batik pieces long sides together to make one long unit. Repeat to make a total of four units. Stitch one unit to the right end of each of the 2½" x 15" tan strips and the 2½" x 17" tan strips. Noting orientation, sew the shorter strips to the sides of the quilt center. Stitch the longer strips to the top and bottom. Press seams toward the border after adding each strip.

3. Layer the quilt top right side up on top of the batting and the wrong side of the backing. Baste the layers together and quilt as desired. Trim the backing and batting even with the quilt top.

4. Bind using the remaining 2½" tan strips. (See *General Quilting Directions*.)

Quilt Layout Diagram

Decorative Curio Cabinet

A Gala of Fruit Wall Hanging Companion Piece

Materials

- White tone-on-tone fabric (size of choice)
- *DecoArt* Americana SoSoft Fabric Acrylics: Antique Gold, Avocado Green, Brown, Buttermilk, Burnt Sienna, Cadmium Yellow, Canary Yellow, Crimson, Olive Green, White, Wine
- *DecoArt* Americana Acrylics: Buttermilk
- *Loew-Cornell* White Nylon ⅛", ¼", ⅜", and ½" angular flat (Series 793), #6/0 liner (Series 801), #2 round (Series 795)
- *DecoArt* Americana Transparent Medium
- *DecoArt* DuraClear Varnish, Matte
- *Miscellaneous:* freezer paper (waxed), heavy foam core or cardboard, iron, masking tape, rolling pin, sandpaper, soft cloth, stylus, tracing paper, transfer paper, waxed-paper palette, wet palette or small paint cups for mixes

Note: The pineapple is painted using the same fabric as for the wall hanging. Once painted, it may be attached to another surface, such as a panel for a cabinet from a home décor store.

Preparation

1. Basecoat wooden panel with Buttermilk. When dry, lightly sand. Wipe off dust.

2. Prepare the fabric and transfer the pattern from the Pattern Section in the same manner as for the wall hanging.

Painting

Note: Review Techniques section for the wall hanging before beginning this project.

Pineapple

1. Base the entire pineapple shape with Antique Gold + Cadmium Yellow + Canary Yellow. Let dry. Re-pattern the crosshatch areas.

2. Drybrush the light area in the center of each diamond with Cadmium Yellow + Canary Yellow. Shade around each section with Antique Gold + Burnt Sienna. If needed, deepen the shading with a thin float of Brown. Paint a dip-dot of Brown in the center of each diamond. Around each dot, paint four comma strokes using Canary Yellow + White.

Leaves

1. Base with Canary Yellow + a touch of Avocado Green. Shade with Avocado Green + Antique Gold. Deepen dark areas with Olive Green + a touch of Brown. Highlight with Base mix + Buttermilk. Reinforce highlight with Buttermilk.

Using the liner, paint the vein lines with Olive Green + a touch of Brown.

2. Accent with Crimson + Brown, or Wine.

Finishing

1. Apply a liberal coat of matte varnish to the wooden panel. While wet, carefully lay the pineapple on the surface. Lay a piece of waxed freezer paper over the pineapple, (shiny side facing the pineapple) and smooth out fabric, being careful not to pull it out of shape. You may use a rolling pin. Remove freezer paper and apply a coat of varnish to the entire pineapple. Allow to dry.

2. Insert the panel in the cabinet.

Elegant Roses and Hydrangeas Table Runner

Donna Dewberry

In this design, the fabric becomes the shading and depth of the elements instead of just the surface!

Materials

- 1⅔ yards of brown fern batik
- *Plaid* FolkArt Fabric Dimensional Paint: Pearl Champagne, Pearl White
- *Plaid* FolkArt Fabric Paint (Brush on): Wicker White
- *Plaid* FolkArt OneStroke Brushes For Paper/Fabric: #12 flat (Get Started! Fabric Brush Set) and #16 flat (Fabric Brush Set)
- *Plaid* FolkArt Floating Medium; Fabric Spray Medium; OneStroke Painting Forms Set (includes T-shirt form)
- *Miscellaneous:* chalk, foam plates (palette), cardboard, paper towels, pencil, plastic wrap, tracing paper, transfer paper

Preparation

1. Always wash and dry fabric prior to painting so that any sizing or conditioners remaining from manufacturing are removed. Do not use any fabric softeners, as they tend to prevent the paint from absorbing into the fibers. Iron the fabric if necessary, and attach to the T-shirt form or piece of cardboard that has been covered with plastic wrap.

2. Cut one 17" x 57" lengthwise brown fern batik strip for painting. (Reserve remaining fabric for quilting instructions.)

3. If desired, trace and transfer the design from the Pattern Section. Repeat various parts of the pattern, continuing the design to form a vine. Another option is to use a piece of chalk and draw the main vine. Use circles to mark the placement of the roses and the main cluster of hydrangeas. This option allows you to create your own version of the design.

Techniques

- Depending on how much of a perfectionist you are, painting on fabric can be fun or frustrating. If you are a perfectionist, the rough edges caused by the absorbency of the fabric will bother you, but if you permit the fabric to become part of the design, you won't notice the raw edges. So relax and allow the imperfections to create this beautiful design.
- *Color mixtures.* Mix a few drops of FolkArt Fabric Spray Medium with a puddle of FolkArt Floating Medium. The Floating Medium thickens the consistency of the Spray Medium. The combination of the two is the Medium referred to when double-loading the brush, and is the transparent color of the strokes.
- *Loading the brushes.* Moisten the brushes first with water and blot well on a paper towel. Load the brush with Medium and then dip one corner into Wicker White. Blend the paint and medium until the color on the brush fades from white on one corner to clear on the other corner. Squirt a puddle of Dimensional Pearl White and Dimensional Pearl Champagne next to each other, and stroke the brush next to these puddles, allowing the white corner to touch both puddles. Load the brush this way for every stroke of the design, making sure the color stays on only one side of the brush. If the paint starts to encroach on the other corner, wipe that corner on a paper towel and pick up some Medium.

Painting

Note: Refer to the Worksheet on page 57 as you paint.

Vine and roses

1. Load the #16 flat with Medium and Wicker White; add Pearl White and Pearl Champagne. Using the chisel edge of the brush and leading with the Medium corner, paint the main vine. Add a few tendrils coming off the vine.

2. Using the flat side of the same brush, keep the color to the outer edge, and paint the roses. Add a few buds here and there. Paint the buds by first painting the center bud strokes and then adding a few comma strokes.

Large leaves and one-stroke leaves

1. Load the #16 flat with Medium and Wicker White; add Pearl White and Pearl Champagne. Using the flat side of the brush, keep the color to the outer edge and paint the large leaves.

2. Load the #12 flat with Medium and Wicker White; add Pearl White and Pearl Champagne. Using the flat side of the brush, keep the color to the outer edge and paint smaller versions of the large leaves and some one-stroke leaves.

Painted panel

Hydrangeas and scrolls

1. Load the #16 flat with Medium and Wicker White; add Pearl White and Pearl Champagne. Using the flat side of the brush, keep the color to the outer edge and paint the clusters of hydrangeas. Start by painting a few partial flowers around the outer edges of the clusters and fill in with complete flowers toward the center of the clusters. Add trailing petals here and there to add interest and graceful curves.

2. Using the same brush, add the long scrolls throughout the design.

Dimensional details

1. Using the tip of the bottle of Dimensional Pearl Champagne, dot the centers of the hydrangeas and outline one side of a few leaves.

2. Using the tip of the bottle of Dimensional Pearl White, add a few curls throughout the design.

Finishing

Allow the paint to completely dry. Heat-set the paint in a clothes dryer for 20 minutes. Set the temperature on the dryer to the proper setting for the type of fabric.

Painted panel

Elegant Roses and Hydrangeas Worksheet

Shell Stroke

Start   End

Add more petals

Completed outer skirt

Center Bud

Start   End

Start   End

Start   Start

End

End

Start   End

1

2

Add center bud

Add comma strokes around bud

One-Stroke Leaves

Start   End

Start   End

Pull stems into leaves using the chisel edge of the brush

Large leaves

End

Start

End

Start

Start   End

Start

End

Outline one side of leaf using Dimensional Pearl Champagne

Scrolls and Curls

Push

Push

Lift

Hydrangeas

End

Start   End

Start

Start   End

Lift

Lift

Connect all petals in the center

Dot the center with Dimensional Pearl Champagne

Add trailing petals

Add dimensional curls using the tip of the bottle of Dimension Pearl White

Quilting
Table runner pieced and quilted
by Cindy Gensamer

Skill level: Beginner
Finished table runner size: 20" x 59"

Materials

Note: Yardage is based on 42" wide useable fabric.
- Painted brown batik panel trimmed to 16½" x 55½"
- ¼ yard white tonal fabric
- Remaining brown fern batik (for borders and binding)
- 28" x 66" piece of backing fabric
- 28" x 66" piece of batting
- Thread in colors to match fabrics
- Basic sewing and rotary cutting supplies

Cutting

From the white tonal, cut:
Four 1" x 42" strips (for dimensional border)

From the brown fern batik, cut:
Six 2½" x 60" lengthwise strips; recut one strip into two 2½" x 16½" (for borders and binding)

Assembly

1. *Dimensional border.* Sew three 1" x 42" white tonal strips short ends together to make one long strip. Cut two 55½" lengths. From the remaining white tonal strip, cut two 16½" lengths. Fold each strip in half lengthwise wrong sides together and press. Lay the shorter strips on each short end of the center painted panel, lining up the raw edges, and baste in place using a ⅛" seam allowance. Attach the longer strips to the sides in the same manner. (This folded border will remain on top of the center panel.)

2. *Outer border.* With right sides together, stitch a 2½" x 16½" brown batik strip to each short end of the center panel. Press seams toward border strips. Sew a 2½" x 60" brown batik strip to the remaining sides of the center panel. Press seams toward the outer borders.

3. Lay the runner right side up on top of the batting and the wrong side of the backing. Baste the layers together and quilt as desired. Trim the backing and batting even with the runner top.

4. Bind using the remaining brown batik strips. (See *General Quilting Directions.*)

Elegant Roses and Hydrangeas Serving Platter

Elegant Roses and Hydrangeas Table Runner Companion Piece

3. There is no pattern for this piece. It's best to adapt the design to fit your unique platter. Trace the shape of the surface onto a piece of paper, and practice painting the design until you get something you like. Then, keep the paper sample close while you paint on the surface. Remember to be loose and have fun.

Techniques

Moisten the brush with Clear Medium and then dip one corner into Wicker White. Blend the paint and medium until the color on the brush fades from the white on one corner to clear on the other corner. Tip the white corner of the brush into Pearl White. Load the brush this way for every stroke of the design, making sure the color stays on only one side of the brush. If the paint starts to encroach on the other corner, wipe that corner on a paper towel and pick up some Clear Medium.

Painting

Refer to the painting instructions for the fabric design, using Clear Medium instead of Fabric Medium.

Materials

Cream-colored ceramic platter or serving dish
Plaid FolkArt Enamels: Burnt Umber, Pearl White, Wicker White
Plaid FolkArt OneStroke Get Started Brush Set for Glass and Ceramics (includes a ¾" flat and #12 flat)
Plaid FolkArt Enamels Clear Medium
Miscellaneous: foam plates (palette), paper towels, plastic wrap, tracing paper, transfer paper

Finishing

Allow the surface to air-dry for 21 days, or bake. To bake, allow the surface to air-dry for one hour. Place in a cool oven and heat to 350°F. Bake for 30 minutes, and let cool.

Important note: Although the FolkArt Enamel Paints are nontoxic, they are for decorative painting purposes and are not suitable for coming in contact with food. Cover painted surfaces with plastic wrap if you will be using them for food service. Hand-wash platter or place in the top rack of the dishwasher.

~~P~~reparation

1. Wash the piece thoroughly, removing any dust. Let dry.
2. *Antiquing.* Load a large flat brush with Clear Medium. ~~Lo~~ad half the brush with Burnt Umber. Brush the Burnt Umber ~~alo~~ng the outside edge of the platter, dabbing it into the ~~mol~~ded areas. Soften by patting with a paper towel. If neces-~~sar~~y, dampen a clean paper towel and wipe off any antiquing ~~wh~~ich may have spread onto the inner portion of the platter. ~~Let~~ dry before continuing.

Old Strokes Quilted Throw

Andy Jones

This style of coffeepot is iconic in the world of folk art. Here, the Decorative Arts Collection Museum's nearly 200-year-old coffeepot is depicted in a more "painterly" fashion. Remember, folk art changes over time, so never be afraid to experiment!

Materials

- ⅔ yard cream tonal fabric (for coffeepot panel)
- ¾ yard burgundy tonal fabric (for painted corner blocks; reserve remaining for quilting instructions)
- *Plaid* FolkArt Fabric Paint (Brush On): Asphaltum, Autumn Leaves, Berry Wine, Engine Red, Lemon Custard, Licorice, Wicker White, Yellow Ochre
- *Plaid* FolkArt Acrylics: Butter Pecan, Lipstick Red
- *Plaid* FolkArt Artists' Pigments: Burnt Umber
- *Silver Brush Ltd.* Ruby Satin #8 and #12 filbert (Series 2503S), #12 bright (Series 2502S); Golden Natural #2 script (Series 2007S), ¾" square wash (Series 2028S); PCM Faux Finish 1" glaze/varnish and 3" basecoat brush (Series 1414S)
- *Plaid* FolkArt Textile Medium
- *Miscellaneous:* blue painter's tape, large support (wood or heavy cardboard), paper towels, pencil, stylus, tracing paper, freezer paper (waxed), white and gray transfer paper

Preparation

1. Wash, dry, and iron the fabric. Do not use fabric softener, dryer sheets, or spray starch.

2. Tape a piece of waxed freezer paper (waxy-side up) on a large support. Place the fabric on the freezer paper and tape in place.

3. Trace pattern from Pattern Section and transfer the outlines of the coffeepot to the fabric. Do not transfer the stroke design at this time.

Painting

Note: This image was painted traditionally and then a loose overpainting was added. If you prefer your folk art more traditional, simply eliminate overpainting steps.

Refer to Worksheet on page 63 as you paint.

Center square

1. Coffeepot. Using the ¾" square wash brush, apply a thin coat of Textile Medium to the coffeepot. You should have no water in your brush as you apply the medium to the fabric.

Thin Engine Red with water + Textile Medium (1:1). Paint along the edges of the coffeepot. Continue brushing this in toward the center of the coffeepot. The goal is to have a gradation of value from strong red at the edge to a lighter red in the center.

Darken the edges by brushing some Berry Wine along the edges and at the seams of the coffeepot. Use loose brushwork to blend the color inward.

While the pot is still wet, add a little Licorice to Berry Wine and add some darker value to the edges, still blending inward.

Using the #2 script, add some highlights to the edges of the lid, the joint on the spout, the joint at the bottom of the pot and the base, and on the handle. The first highlight is a mix of Engine Red + Autumn Leaves. If desired, lighten this mix with Lemon Custard, and add additional highlights. Let dry completely.

2. Transfer the stroke design to the coffeepot with the white transfer paper.

3. Ball flowers. Using the #12 filbert, form the ball flowers with a warm gray mix of Butter Pecan + Wicker White + Burnt Umber. While wet, pick up a little Burnt Umber and Licorice on one side of the brush and shade the dark side of the ball flower form, quickly blending into the flower.

Load the #8 filbert with Asphaltum, and paint the dark overstrokes on the ball flowers. Paint the light strokes with Wicker White.

Using the #8 filbert, paint the dark strokes with a mix of Licorice + Burnt Umber (1:1), and the yellow strokes with Yellow Ochre. Let dry completely.

4. Overpainting. Using the 3" basecoat brush, wet the fabric with water. Be sure to brush some water over the coffeepot as well.

Thin Lipstick Red with water + a touch of Textile Medium. Using the 1" glaze/varnish brush, dab some color next to the coffeepot, allowing the color to bleed out. You may need to add more color or more water to get a nice bleed of color and a mottled appearance. Be sure some of this bleeds inside the coffeepot as well. Add a little Berry Wine to the red and brush next to the coffeepot. Let the fabric partially dry and add some more thinned red.

When the fabric is dry, use the 1" glaze/varnish brush and apply streaks of Lipstick Red here and there over the coffeepot and the background. Let dry completely.

5. Repaint the ball flowers using the same color and technique as in step 3 above, but don't completely cover the red which may be on the stroke design.

Corner squares

1. Cut one 9" x 42" strip of burgundy tonal fabric; recut into four 9" squares.

2. Paint ball flower designs following the same technique as described in step 3 for the coffeepot.

3. When dry, use the 1" glaze/varnish brush to lightly brush some Lipstick Red over the design, where desired.

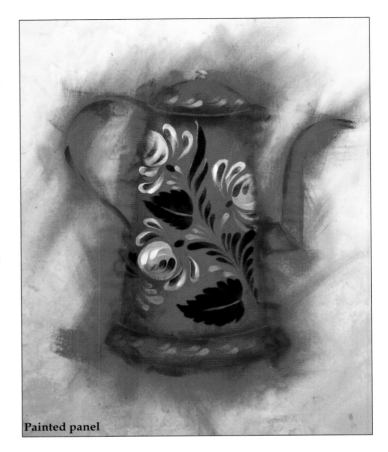

Painted panel

Painted panel

Painted panel

Painted panel

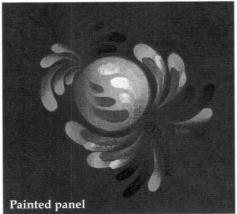

Painted panel

Old Strokes Worksheet

Quilting

**Quilt designed and quilted
by *Cindy Gensamer;*
pieced by *Audrey Hydrick***

Skill level: Beginner/Intermediate
Finished wall hanging size: 44" x 47"

Materials

Note: Yardage is based on 42" wide useable fabric.
- One painted coffeepot panel trimmed to 21½" x 24½"
- Four painted corner panels trimmed to 8" x 8"
- ½ yard tan print fabric
- Reserved burgundy tonal fabric
- 1¼ yards black tonal fabric (includes binding)
- 50" x 53" piece of backing fabric
- 50" x 53" piece of batting
- Thread in colors to match fabrics
- Basic sewing and rotary cutting supplies

Cutting

From the tan print, cut:
Four 3" x 42" strips; recut into fourteen 3" x 8 ½" pieces and four 3" x 5 ½" pieces

From the burgundy tonal, cut:
Five 3" x 42" strips; recut into sixteen 3" x 8 ½" pieces and two 3" x 5 ½" pieces

From the black tonal, cut:
Five 3½" x 42" strips for the outer border
Five 2½" x 42" strips for the binding
Five 1½" x 42" strips; recut into two 1½" x 38½" strips, two 1½" x 24½" strips, and four 11½" x 8" pieces.

Directions

Note: Use a ¼" seam allowance throughout. Sew all pieces with right sides together and raw edges even, using matching thread. Press seams toward the darker fabric unless otherwise indicated.

1. *Side segments.* Following **Diagram 1** and using 3" x 8½" pieces, sew five tan print and four burgundy tonal pieces alternately together in three rows of three pieces each. Press row seams in opposing directions, then stitch the rows together to complete one 8" x 24½" segment. Repeat to make a second segment.

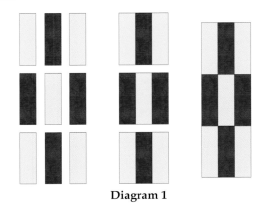

Diagram 1

2. *Top and bottom segments.* Referring to **Diagram 2**, gather together four 3" x 8½" burgundy tonal pieces, two 3" x 8½" tan print pieces, two 3" x 5½" tan print pieces, and one 3" x 5½" burgundy tonal piece. With the shorter pieces in the center, sew the pieces alternately together in three rows of three pieces each. Press seams in opposing directions, then stitch the rows together to make one 8" x 21½" segment. Repeat to make a second segment.

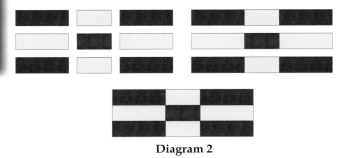

Diagram 2

Assembly

Note: Refer to the **Quilt Layout Diagram** for steps 1 through 4.

1. Sew a 1½" x 24½" black strip, then a segment from step 1, to each long side of the coffeepot panel. Press seams toward the black strips.

2. Stitch a 1½" x 38½" black strip to the top and another to the bottom of the coffeepot section.

3. Sew the top and bottom segments between two 1½" x 8" black pieces and two painted corner panels. Stitch one to the top and another to the bottom of the coffeepot section to complete the 38½" x 41½" quilt center.

4. Sew the 3½" x 42" black tonal strips short ends together to make a long strip. Cut two 44½" lengths and two 41½" lengths. Sew the shorter strips to each side of the quilt center and the longer strips to the top and bottom.

5. Layer the quilt top right side up on top of the batting and the wrong side of the backing. Baste the layers together and quilt as desired. Trim the backing and batting even with the quilt top.

6. Bind using the five 2½" x 42" black strips. (See *General Quilting Directions.*)

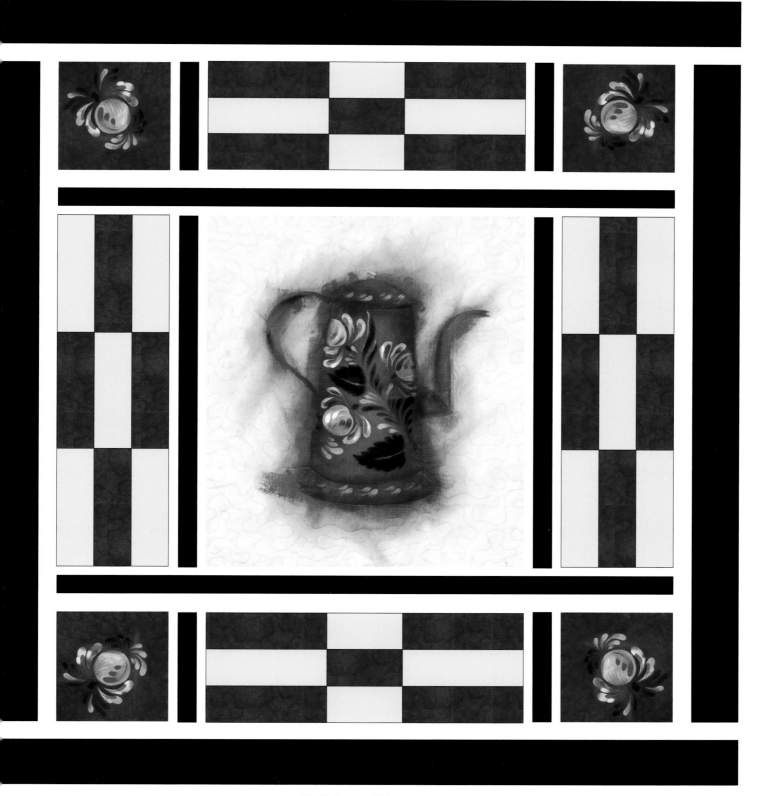

Quilt Layout Diagram

Recipe Box

Old Strokes Quilted Throw Companion Piece

Materials

- Salt box*
- *Plaid* FolkArt Acrylics: Asphaltum, Butter Pecan, Licorice, Lipstick Red, Wicker White
- *Plaid* FolkArt Artists' Pigments: Burnt Umber, Pure Black, Sap Green, True Burgundy, Yellow Ochre
- *Silver Brush Ltd.* Ruby Satin #8 and #12 filbert (Series 2503S), #12 bright (Series 2502S); Golden Natural #2 script (Series 2007S), ¾" square wash (Series 2028S); PCM Faux Finish 1" glaze/varnish and 3" basecoat brush (Series 1414S)
- *3M* Scotch-Brite Heavy Duty Scrub Sponge (green)
- *Miscellaneous:* clear acrylic spray, liquid dish detergent, palette knife, paper towels, sandpaper, satin waterbased varnish, stylus, tracing paper, white and gray transfer paper

* This salt box is an antique reproduction purchased at an online auction. You can adapt the design to any surface of choice.

Preparation

1. Load the 1" glaze/varnish with Lipstick Red and basecoat the box. Let dry, and apply a second coat.

2. Sideload the ¾" square wash with water and True Burgundy. Shade the edges of the box. Darken the True Burgundy edge of the brush by stroking into some Sap Green. Brush the color along the edge of the box, and lightly blend into the box using a slip-slapping motion. The edges should appear darker and fade into the Lipstick Red. Let dry.

3. Trace pattern from Pattern Section and transfer the design onto the box.

Painting

1. Using the #12 filbert, form the ball flowers with a warm gray mix of Butter Pecan + Wicker White + Burnt Umber. While wet, pick up a little Burnt Umber and Pure Black on one side of the brush and shade the dark side of the ball flower form, quickly blending it into the flower. Let dry.

2. Load the # 8 filbert with Asphaltum, and paint the dark overstrokes on the ball flowers. Paint the light strokes with Wicker White.

3. Using the #8 filbert, paint the dark strokes with a mix of Licorice + Burnt Umber (1:1), and the yellow strokes with Yellow Ochre. Let dry completely.

Finishing

1. When the design is dry, varnish with three coats of satin waterbased varnish.

2. *Antiquing.* The antiquing process adds a nice aged quality to the finished piece. Mix Licorice + Apshaltum (1:1). To this mix, add an equal volume of dishwashing liquid and mix thoroughly with a palette knife. The soap makes the paint film softer and easier to remove. Using the ¾" square wash brush, apply a thin coat of the antiquing mixture to the box, and let dry. To remove the antiquing, begin to scrub the antiquing off using the heavy-duty scrubbing pad. If the antiquing is difficult to remove, lightly wipe the surface with a damp paper towel and continue scrubbing. When you are pleased with the results, allow the antiquing to dry for several hours.

3. Finish with several coats of clear acrylic spray.

Holiday Bell Pull

*Lynne Deptula and
Judy Diephouse*

Poinsettias bring such joy to the holiday home! They are lovely to look at, delightful to paint, and reward you with unsurpassed beauty on a snowy winter day.

Materials

- 1⅓ yards of burgundy tonal fabric (Cut one 9" x 27" piece for painting; reserve remaining fabric for quilting instructions)
- Café curtain rod cut to desired length
- *DecoArt* Americana SoSoft Fabric Acrylics: Bright Coral, Canary Yellow, Crimson, Dark Rose, Navy Blue, Ocean Blue, Olive Green, Pine Green, Red Pepper, Santa Red, Wine, Yellow Green
- *DecoArt* Americana SoSoft Fabric Acrylics (Metallic): Glorious Gold
- *DecoArt* Americana SoSoft Fabric Acrylics (Neons): Neon Red
- *DecoArt* SoSoft Transparent Medium
- *Loew-Cornell* La Corneille Golden Taklon Jackie Shaw #2 liner (Series JS), #4 and #10 shader (Series 7300), #1 liner (Series 7350), ¾" glaze/wash (Series 7550)
- *Miscellaneous:* plastic watercolor tray (or other rigid, smooth plastic surface), ruler, stylus, tape, tracing paper, white graphite paper

Preparation

1. Wash the fabric in warm soapy water, and rinse thoroughly to remove all sizing. Do not use fabric softener. Let dry, and press well. Do not use spray starch.

2. Tape the fabric to the plastic watercolor tray surface.

3. Trace pattern from Pattern Section, and transfer onto fabric with white graphite paper and a stylus using as little pressure as possible.

Painting

Poinsettias

1. Undercoat all poinsettia petals with the ¾" glaze/wash brush and a mix of Transparent Medium + Red Pepper (1:3). Separate, and shade across the base of all the petals, with a sideload of Wine. Highlight the outside edges of every petal with a sideload of Bright Coral. Further highlight the edges of some of the top petals with a sideload of Neon Red or Dark Rose. Apply the paint generously, as it fades when it dries.

2. Add a soft glow to the entire poinsettia using a sheer glaze of Crimson. Deepen the glaze on the back poinsettia with a sheer layer of Wine. Reapply spot highlights of Dark Rose to some petal edges, giving the poinsettia "pops" of highlight.

Poinsettia berry centers

Smudge in small circles for the poinsettia centers using the #2 liner and Olive Green. Sideload the #4 shader with Yellow Green, and highlight each poinsettia berry using small C-strokes. With the #1 liner, further highlight each berry with a loose outline of Yellow Green. Finish the center with a dot of Neon Red and tiny scattered dots of Canary Yellow.

Holly leaves and loose stem lines

1. Underoat the holly leaves using the #10 shader, and a mix of Pine Green + Navy Blue + Transparent Medium (2:1:1). Shade the base of each holly leaf with a sideload of brush-mixed undercoat color + a touch of Crimson.

2. Using the #1 liner and Pine Green, pull thin vein lines and loose stems connecting to the berries. Highlight the veins and stems with

hit-and-miss touches of Olive Green. Highlight the outside edges of all leaves with a sideload of Pine Green, and add additional highlights to outside edges of front leaves using a sideload of Olive Green.

3. Tint some of the edges of the holly leaves with either Pine Green + Navy Blue + Ocean Blue (3:1:1) or Pine Green + Ocean Blue (2:1). Loosely outline the holly leaves with the #1 liner and Olive Green.

Berries

Undercoat the berries with the #4 shader and one coat of Santa Red + Dark Rose (1:1). Allow the background to show through so that it acts as the shading color. Highlight the outside edge of each berry with a sideload of Dark Rose. Add additional highlights to some of the berries with a sideload of Canary Yellow. Highlight each berry with a dot of Glorious Gold.

Tendrils

Using the #1 liner and Glorious Gold, pull loose tendrils from the design sections.

Cafe rod (optional)

Paint the rod with a burgundy paint as close to the color of the fabric as possible. Dab Glorious Gold on the ends of the rod as seen in the photo.

Painted panel

Holiday Bell Pull Worksheet

Quilting

Quilt designed, pieced, and quilted
by **Cindy Gensamer**

Skill level: Beginner/Intermediate
Finished size: 11" x 31"

Materials

Note: Yardage is based on 42" wide useable fabric.
- Painted panel trimmed to 8½" x 26½"
- Remaining burgundy tonal fabric (includes binding, backing, and hanging sleeve)
- ⅓ yd. gold tonal fabric
- *Mount Redoubt Designs* "Poinsettia Elegance" Crystal Kit, #MRD035
- 17" x 37" piece of batting
- Thread in colors to match fabric
- Gold metallic thread (optional)
- Basic sewing and rotary cutting supplies

Cutting

From the gold tonal, cut:
One 3" x 42" strip; recut into eight 3" squares
Two 1" x 42" strips

From the burgundy tonal, cut:
One 17" x 37" strip (for backing)
One 6" x 42" strip; recut into one 6" x 8" piece (for hanging sleeve) and one 5½" x 13⅕" piece (for bottom section)
Three 2½" x 42" strips (for binding)
Two 1½" x 42" strips (for borders)

Assembly

Note: Use a ¼" seam allowance throughout unless otherwise indicated. Sew all pieces with right sides together and raw edges even, using matching thread.

1. *Prairie points.* Following **Diagram 1**, fold each 3" gold tonal square diagonally in half, wrong sides together, then in half again, pressing as you go.

Diagram 1

2. *Bottom section.* Fold the 5½" x 13½" burgundy piece in half widthwise as shown in **Diagram 2**. Cut diagonally from the bottom left corner to the top right corner. Open one triangle piece and trim 2⅜" in from each end. (*Note:* This trimmed triangle piece measures 8½" wide along the top edge.)

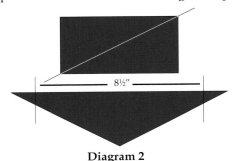

Diagram 2

Referring to **Diagram 3**, pin the prairie points to the right side of the bottom section, along the top edge, lining up the raw edges and overlapping the points. Make sure the points are evenly spaced and the beginning point and ending point extend beyond the bottom section. Baste in place using a ⅛" seam allowance.

Diagram 3

3. With right sides together and using a ¼" seam allowance, sew the 8½" x 26½" painted panel to the bottom section. Press seam toward the painted panel.

4. *Borders.* Stitch each 1" x 42" gold tonal strip lengthwise to a 1½" x 42" burgundy tonal strip. Press seams toward the burgundy fabric. Sew a pieced strip to each long side of the panel as shown in the **Bell Pull Diagrams**. Line the straight edge of a rotary ruler along the raw edge of the bottom section, and trim the pieced border strips even with the bottom of the bell pull.

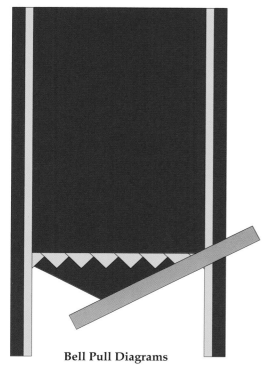

Bell Pull Diagrams

5. Lay the bell pull right side up on top of the batting and wrong side of the backing. Baste the layers together and quilt as desired. (The featured project used gold metallic thread to outline the painted poinsettia motifs and a burgundy thread for the background.)

6. Bind using the three 2½" x 42" burgundy tonal strips. (See *General Quilting Directions*.)

7. Attach the crystals to the flower centers.

8. *Hanging sleeve.* Referring to **Diagram 4** and using the 6" x 8" burgundy tonal piece, fold the short edges under ¼", wrong sides together and press. Fold again, press, and sew a straight seam to hem the folds. Fold the strip lengthwise, wrong sides together, aligning the raw edges, and stitch together using a ½" seam allowance. Press the seam allowance open.

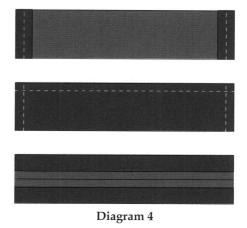

Diagram 4

Center the sleeve on the back of the bell pull under the top binding with the open seam against the backing. Hand-stitch the top of the sleeve to the back. Smooth the sleeve downward along the quilt back, then make a ½" fold along its length to create a pleat. Leaving the pleat intact, pin the sleeve bottom to the bell pull and hand-sew in place. (This allows space for the curtain rod.) Stitch the back side edges of the sleeve to the bell pull, leaving the front edges open for inserting the curtain rod.

Holiday Teapot

Holiday Bell Pull Companion Piece

Materials

- *Painter's Paradise* Metal Tea Kettle, # 897152 (8" x 3½") (www.paintersparadise.com)
- *DecoArt* Americana Acrylics: Alizarin Crimson, Antique Maroon, Antique Teal, Avocado, Black Green, Black Plum, Cadmium Yellow, Cranberry Wine, Deep Midnight Blue, Deep Teal, Desert Turquoise, Hauser Dark Green, Hauser Light Green, Napa Red, Peony Pink, Santa Red, Tomato Red, True Red
- *DecoArt* Dazzling Metallics: Copper, Emperor's Gold, Glorious Gold, Splendid Gold
- *Loew-Cornell* La Corneille Golden Taklon Jackie Shaw #2 liner (Series JS), #4 and #10 shader (Series 7300), #1 liner (Series 7350), ¾" glaze/wash (Series 7550)
- *DecoArt* Americana Acrylic Sealer/Finisher, Matte
- *RUST-OLEUM* Light Gray Automobile Primer
- *Miscellaneous:* blue painter's tape, eraser, palette, paper towels, ruler, stylus, tracing paper, white graphite paper

Preparation

1. Wash and thoroughly dry the teapot.
2. Spray the teapot with Light Gray Auto Primer. Let dry for several days.
3. Basecoat the entire teapot with a mix of Antique Teal + Deep Midnight Blue (1:1). Let dry completely.
4. Trace pattern from Pattern Section, and using white graphite paper and a stylus, transfer the pattern onto the teapot as lightly as possible.
5. Tape off a 1″ band around the bottom of the teapot. Basecoat the band around the bottom of the teapot and the band on the lid with a mix of Napa Red + Antique Maroon (1:1). Outline with a line of Glorious Gold.

Painting

Note: Refer to the Worksheet on page 71 as you paint.

Poinsettias

1. Undercoat the poinsettia petals with a ¾″ glaze/wash brush and Tomato Red. Sideload the brush with a mix of Napa Red + Antique Maroon (1:1), and separate the petals. Highlight the outside edges of all petals with a sideload of Santa Red. Sideload a mix of the Napa Red + Antique Maroon + a touch of Black Plum (1:1:touch), and reinforce the shading in the darkest V-shadows. Highlight the outside edges of the top petals with a sideload of Peony Pink. Repeat several times to achieve a strong highlight.
2. Use the #1 liner and thinned Peony Pink to pull the thin vein lines into some of the poinsettia petals.
3. Glaze the entire poinsettia with a thinned application of True Red to create a warm glow.

Poinsettia berry centers

Smudge in small circles for the poinsettia berry centers using the #2 JS liner and Avocado. Sideload the corner of the #4 shader with Hauser Light Green, and highlight the berries with small C-strokes. Using the #1 liner, further highlight the berries with a loose outline of Hauser Light Green. Finish the center with a large dot of Santa Red and tiny scattered dots of Cadmium Yellow.

Holly leaves and loose stem lines

1. Undercoat the holly leaves with the #10 shader and Hauser Dark Green. Shade the base of each holly leaf with a sideload of Black Green.
2. Using the #1 liner, pull thin vein lines and paint the loose stems connecting to the berries with Hauser Dark Green. Highlight the vein lines and stems with hit-and-miss touches of Hauser Light Green. Highlight all edges of all leaves with a sideload of Deep Teal.
3. Tint some edges of the holly leaves with a soft sideload of either Hauser Light Green or Desert Turquoise. Reinforce the shading on the leaves with an additional sideload of Black Green.

Berries

Undercoat the berries with one coat of Peony Pink using the #4 shader. Apply shading to one side of each berry with a sideload mix of Cranberry Wine + Alizarin Crimson (1:1). Highlight the opposite edge of each berry with a float of Peony Pink. Float an additional highlight on some of the berries with Cadmium Yellow. Dot a highlight on each berry with Emperor's Gold.

Tendrils

Using the #1 liner and Emperor's Gold, line loose tendrils from the design sections.

Faux gold leaf edging

Tape off the top and bottom edges of the teapot, the edges of the handle, and a ½″ band on the spout with blue painter's tape. Using a crumpled paper towel, apply splotchy layers of the following colors: Emperor's Gold, Copper, and Splendid Gold. Paint a line on the bottom edge of the spout band with the #1 liner and a mix of Napa Red + Antique Maroon (1:1).

Strokework trim

1. Using the #1 liner and Emperor's Gold, paint the curls and comma strokes on the teapot bands. Make sure the strokes follow the contours of the curls. Let dry completely.
2. Create a softened finish by slip-slapping a thinned Black Plum glaze over the trim area with the ¾″ wash brush.

Finishing

1. Erase any visible pattern lines.
2. Spray two or three thin layers of matte sealer; let cure 24 hours between applications.

Sunrise Pillow

Ronnie Bringle

The crowing of a rooster is such a homey, relaxing sound.
I love to paint them in all their glorious colors!

Materials

- ⅔ yard medium green tonal fabric (the featured pillow uses a green batik)
- *Chroma, Inc.* Jo Sonja's Artists' Colours: Brown Earth, Burnt Umber, Carbon Black, Celadon, Indian Red Oxide, Napthol Red Light, Olive Green, Paynes Grey, Raw Sienna, Smoked Pearl, Yellow Green, Yellow Light
- *Scharff Brushes* Golden Taklon #0 and #1 Dresden liner (Series 455); #4, #6, and #10 Bringle oval blender (Series #1440); #2, #4, and #8 Bringle round blender (Series 1450)
- *Chroma, Inc.* Jo Sonja's Textile Medium
- *Saral* Transfer Paper, white
- *Miscellaneous supplies:* chalk*, pencil, plastic wrap, pressing cloth, rigid surface, small container for medium, stylus, tape, tracing paper
- *Optional

Preparation

1. Wash, dry, and iron the fabric. Do not use fabric softener, dryer sheets, or spray starch. Cut a 22″ square.

2. Trace pattern from Pattern Section and transfer the design to the fabric using the white transfer paper, or chalk the back of the pattern and transfer onto the fabric.

3. Place the fabric on a rigid surface covered smoothly with plastic wrap. When the fabric is smooth and taut, tape it in place.

Painting

Note: On the palette, mix Yellow Light + Raw Sienna (1:1). This is Color Mix #1. Mix a little Textile Medium into each puddle of color on the palette, or squeeze some Textile Medium into a small container and pick up on the brush as you use each color.

Refer to the Worksheet on page 79 as you paint this project.

Background

1. *Hills.* Drybrush the hills with the #10 oval blender and Olive Green + Yellow Light. Keep this application very subtle, and don't strive for complete coverage.

2. *Sun.* Using the #10 oval blender, paint the sun, blending Yellow Light and Napthol Red Light. Repeat several times. Finish by brushing on a glaze of Textile Medium + Napthol Red Light for the most intense red. Paint the sun rays with Mix #1 using the chisel edge of the #6 oval blender or a liner brush.

Rooster

1. *Body and wings.* Load the #8 round blender with Olive Green and Celadon, and stipple and drybrush the breast and upper legs. Shade by stippling with Olive Green and Paynes Grey. Be sure to stipple some of the darker greens into the neck feathers to provide the proper color between the feathers. Stipple the highlight with a mix of Celadon + Yellow Green.

Using the chisel edge of the #6 oval blender, drybrush the wing with Indian Red Oxide and Raw Sienna. Continue using the chisel edge, and drybrush the red sections of the wing with Napthol Red Light and the yellow sections with Mix #1. Add brighter highlights to the yellow sections by drybrushing with a little Smoked Pearl.

2. *Tail feathers.* With the chisel edge of the #10 oval blender, loosely paint the tail feathers with Raw Sienna. Loosely paint the head and neck feathers with the #6 oval blender and Raw Sienna. Repeat several times, pressing and lifting for fat and thin feathers.

Mix Napthol Red Light + Textile Medium to a glaze consistency, and brush here and there on all the feathers using the #10 oval blender. Mix another glaze with Brown Earth + Textile Medium, and shade the darker areas on the feathers. Allow the green background to show through between the feathers. Don't worry about painting these glazes on each feather, but brush randomly over the entire feather area, even over the background.

With Mix #1, repaint some of the feathers using the chisel edge of the oval blender. Use a liner brush as needed, especially on some of the tips. Repeat this several times. Using a liner, paint just a few Carbon Black accent lines in the shade area on the feathers. Paint the small tail feathers with a liner and Indian Red Oxide. Highlight with Napthol Red Light, and detail just a bit with Carbon Black using a liner brush.

3. *Face, comb, and wattle.* Using the #2 round blender, blend Indian Red Oxide + Napthol Red Light and paint the face, comb, and wattle. Add a little Paynes Grey to the Indian Red Oxide for the darkest shading. Highlight with more Napthol Red Light.

4. *Beak.* Paint the beak with a liner brush and Raw Sienna. Drybrush the shading with the No. 2 round blender and Brown Earth. Using a liner, drybrush the highlight with Mix #1. Paint the tongue with Indian Red Oxide and highlight with Napthol Red Light.

5. *Eye.* Mix a golden color with just a little Napthol Red Light + Raw Sienna, and paint the eye. Shade the top half of the eye with Brown Earth. Paint the pupil and outline the eye with Carbon Black. Paint the sparkle in the eye with Smoked Pearl. Paint a subtle Burnt Umber line above the eye, and highlight above the line with Napthol Red Light. Refer to the detail of the eye on the Worksheet.

6. *Legs.* Dab the lower legs and feet using the #2 round blender and Raw Sienna. Shade by dabbing with Brown Earth. Highlight with dabs of Mix #1. Paint the claws with Carbon Black.

Finishing

When the painting is dry, heat-set using the iron on the cotton setting. Place a clean pressing cloth over the top of the panel and iron for about 15 seconds. Remove the cloth and iron again. Flip the fabric over and iron the back.

Painted panel

Sunrise Worksheet

Quilting
Pillow designed, pieced, and quilted
by **Cindy Gensamer**

Skill level: Intermediate
Finished pillow size: 27″ square

Materials

Note: Yardage is based on 42″ wide useable fabric.
- One painted square trimmed to 20½″ x 20½″
- Ten fat eighths (9″ x 22″) of assorted red, orange, and yellow tonal fabrics
- ¾ yard muslin fabric
- 1⅞ yards dark green print fabric (for back and ruffle)
- Thread in colors to match fabric
- Poly fiberfill
- Basic sewing and rotary cutting supplies

Cutting

From each of the fat eighths, cut:
Two 6″ x 6″ squares

From the muslin fabric, cut:
One 24″ x 24″ square

From the dark green print, cut:
Five 8″ x 42″ strips (for ruffle)
One 22″ x 22″ square (for back)

Directions

Note: Use a ¼″ seam allowance throughout unless otherwise indicated. Sew all pieces with right sides together and raw edges even, using matching thread. Press seams toward the darker fabric.

1. Layer the 20½″ x 20½″ painted square right side up on top of the batting and the wrong side of the 24″ x 24″ piece of muslin fabric. Quilt as desired. (*Note:* The featured pillow was quilted outlining the rooster, feathers, horizon, and sun.) Trim the batting and the backing even with the painted square.

2. *Prairie points.* Following **Diagram 1**, press each 6″ red, orange, and yellow square in half, wrong sides together, then in half again, pressing as you go. Pin five points ranging in color from darkest to lightest, on top of one side of the painted/quilted square so they overlap approximately 2″, and the raw edges of the points are aligned with the raw edge of the painted square as shown in **Diagram 2**. Pin five more points in

the same manner on the adjacent side, only this time in colors ranging from light to dark. Continue around the remaining sides. Baste in place using a ¼″ seam allowance.

3. *Ruffle.* Sew the five 8″ x 42″ dark green print strips, short ends together, to make one long strip. Press under ½″ along one short end, then press the strip lengthwise in half with the wrong sides together. Double-thread a needle, and starting ½″ in from the folded end, use a long basting stitch to sew a scant ¼″ away from the raw edges along the length of the fabric. Do not knot the end. Pull the threads, gathering the fabric evenly until it measures 86″ long, then knot.

Leaving a 3″ tail and starting with the folded end, align the raw edges of the ruffle on top of the pillow top and prairie points. Baste the ruffle to the quilt top using a ¼″ seam allowance. Stop sewing 3″ away from the beginning stitches. Place the end of the ruffle inside the folded end (beginning), so the folded end is on the outside. Trim away excess from the unfolded end to ¼″. Align the raw edges and finish basting the ruffle to the pillow top.

4. Pin the 22″ dark green print square right sides together with the pillow top, prairie points, and ruffle, aligning the raw edges. Stitch around all four sides using a ½″ seam allowance, making sure to leave a 6″ opening for stuffing.

5. Turn right side out and stuff with poly fiberfill. Hand-stitch the opening closed.

Diagram 1

Diagram 2

Papier-Mâché Box

*Sunrise Pillow
Companion Piece*

Preparation

1. Create a Dark Green Mix using Pine Green + a little Carbon Black. Combine the Dark Green Mix with Jo Sonja's All Purpose Sealer (4:1), and base the box lid.

2. Base the box with a mix of Raw Sienna + sealer (4:1). If your box has embossed fruit, paint with the appropriate colors from the palette.

3. Trace pattern from Pattern Section and transfer to lid.

Painting

Rooster

Paint as above for the quilt using the #2 and #4 round blenders and the #4 and #6 oval blenders. Do *not* add any Textile Medium to the paint.

Trim

1. Paint accent line on the lid and bottom band of the box with three coats of Napthol Red Light.

2. Using the #10 flat blender, paint the checks on the lid with one coat of Napthol Red Light

Finishing

1. When completely dry, coat the box and lid with one coat of Clear Glazing Medium. Let dry.

2. Mix Burnt Umber with water to make a glaze, and antique the painted fruit on the box. Immediately wipe away excess with a damp cloth. Let dry completely, and apply a coat of Clear Glazing Medium over the box.

3. Mix matte varnish + gloss varnish (4:1). Apply three or four coats to the box and lid, as desired.

Materials

- Papier-mâché box of choice
- *Chroma, Inc.* Jo Sonja's Artists' Colours: Brown Earth, Burnt Umber, Carbon Black, Celadon, Indian Red Oxide, Napthol Red Light, Olive Green, Paynes Grey, Pine Green, Raw Sienna, Smoked Pearl, Yellow Green, Yellow Light
- *Scharff Brushes* Golden Taklon #0 and #1 Dresden liner (Series 455); #4 and #6 Bringle oval blender (Series #1440); #2 and #4 Bringle round blender (Series 1450); #6 and #10 Bringle flat blender (Series 1460)
- *Chroma, Inc.* Jo Sonja's All Purpose Sealer, Jo Sonja's Clear Glazing Medium, Jo Sonja's Matte Varnish, Jo Sonja's Gloss Varnish
- *Saral* Transfer Paper, white
- *Miscellaneous supplies:* soft cloth, tracing paper, stylus

Indian Peafowl Wall Hanging

Sherry Nelson

The Indian peafowl is one of the most spectacular birds in the avian world. With extraordinary iridescence, complex patterning, and adorned with incredible tail feathers and crest, the bird is a showy subject for quilted fabric paintings.

Materials

- 1 yard light blue tonal
- *Winsor & Newton* Artist's Oils: Burnt Sienna, Cadmium Yellow Pale, French Ultramarine, Ivory Black, Oxide of Chromium, Phthalo Turquoise, Raw Sienna, Raw Umber, Sap Green, Titanium White, Winsor Green, Winsor Red, Winsor Violet
- *Sherry C. Nelson* Red Sable Brushes: #0, #2, #4, #6, and #8 bright (Series 303), #1 round (Series 312), liner brush of choice
- *Delta* Ceramcoat Acrylics: Black
- *Grumbacher* Cobalt Drier (siccative)
- *DecoArt* Americana Acrylic Sealer/Finisher, Matte
- *Miscellaneous:* ballpoint pen, odorless thinner, palette knife, oil paint palette, paper towels, tape, tracing paper, white graphite paper*

Use artist's graphite for oils — not water removable papers created for acrylics.

Preparation

1. Wash with mild detergent. Do not use fabric softener. Let dry.

2. From the light blue fabric, cut one 19" x 29" piece and one 8" x 13" piece.

3. Spray design area with DecoArt Americana Acrylic Sealer/Finisher until fabric is slightly damp. Let surface dry thoroughly.

4. *Transfer design.* Lay fabric flat on a hard surface. Tape design from the Pattern Section on fabric. Slide white graphite under design. Tape tracing paper on top of pattern to protect original design and make transfer more accurate. Carefully transfer all feather lines on bird, including all black marking on wings, and all details on other elements with a ballpoint pen. New graphite paper makes tiny, complex wing shapes more easily visible.

Techniques

- *Using a drier.* Add a fraction of a drop of cobalt siccative, a drying agent, to each patty of oil paint on the palette to speed drying time. Mix each tiny freckle of siccative into a paint patty with a clean palette knife. The color should remain workable on the palette for at least eight hours, then dry within six hours or overnight, depending on particular pigment and humidity.

- *Brush loading and blending.* Load color onto brushes from a loading zone, by pulling a strip of sparse paint from a patty of paint down on the palette. Make mixtures by moving from one loading zone to another, working back and forth. Wipe brush on a paper towel after applying paint to surface, but before beginning to blend. Blend colors *where they meet*, using a dry brush and short strokes. Don't blend randomly; blend *on the line* where colors come together, creating a new value and hue with the blending process. The iridescent quality of feathers is best accomplished with minimal blending. Overblending causes loss of values and clarity.

- *Working on fabric with oils.* Thin oil paint a bit with odorless thinner for each step in order to allow it to move easily on fabric texture. Dip the corner of the brush into thinner and then work it into the various mixes. Thin only as much as you use at a time. Do *not* thin paint with any oily mediums or linseed oil, as this may cause bleed lines beyond the design.

Painting

Note: Refer to the Worksheets on pages 86 and 87 as you paint.

Indian Peafowl
Acrylic detail

Underpaint complex patterns on peafowl wing with Black acrylic. As you work, thin paint slightly with water. Use a #0 bright brush or a #1 round, nothing larger. Rinse brush frequently in water, and squeeze back to a good chisel to make detailing easier. When all acrylic patterning is complete, proceed to the oil steps below.

Crested head feathers

Streak outer end of shaft lines with Ivory Black and the base of shaft lines with Titanium White. Blend a bit with chisel of the brush where values meet.

Feather tufts

1. Dark: Ivory Black. Light: French Ultramarine.
2. Highlight for iridescence: Phthalo Turquoise + Titanium White.

Eye ring and eye

1. Eye ring base: Raw Umber + Titanium White. Eye line and around eye ring base: Ivory Black, narrowing eye ring until it is appropriate width.
2. Eye: Base with Ivory Black. Highlight with Titanium White.

White patches on face

1. Base: Titanium White.
2. Highlight: Titanium White stippling with round brush.

Remaining area of head

1. Base: French Ultramarine.
2. Highlight: Phthalo Turquoise + Titanium White. Paint iridescent feather markings and stipple texture where needed using a #0 bright.

Beak

1. Dark: Raw Umber + Raw Sienna. Light: Raw Sienna + Titanium White.
2. Highlight: Titanium White + Raw Sienna, then Titanium White.

Neck and back

1. Dark: Ivory Black. Light: French Ultramarine. Blend where colors meet.
2. Paint iridescent strokes on neck using Phthalo Turquoise + French Ultramarine + Titanium White with the chisel edge of a #2 bright. Follow growth direction. Highlight some with Phthalo Turquoise + Titanium White and a #0 bright or a round brush. Strokes should appear a bit rough and choppy.

Primaries and primary coverts

1. Base: Ivory Black.
2. Streak in all feather lines with a dirty Phthalo Turquoise + Titanium White mix. Blend top row into bottom edge of neck.

Dirty white feathering at edge of breast

Dark: Raw Sienna + Raw Umber. Light: Raw Sienna + Titanium White. Streak dark area with dirty white. Highlight light area with cleaner white.

Rump (upper back under leaves)

Base: Ivory Black. Add iridescence with French Ultramarine + Sap Green + Titanium White, laying in the rough feather shapes with a #2 bright.

Wing coverts (black-and-white pattern)

1. As perfectly as possible, base every black marking with a liner brush and Black acrylic. When dry, outline around edges and on separation lines where indicated with Raw Sienna or Raw Sienna + Raw Umber and a #4 bright.
2. Base remaining areas between acrylic markings with sparse markings of Titanium White or a dirty brush + Titanium White. When area is completely filled in, highlight most dominant feathers with clean Titanium White and a round brush.

Taileye spots

Note: Paint in same manner as large feather eyespot on the Worksheet.

1. Base the eye of each feather with the following mixes:
Green band: Sap Green + Ivory Black + Winsor Green.
Rusty band: Narrow band of Raw Umber next to green band already completed. Paint remaining area Burnt Sienna + Raw Sienna.
Turquoise band: Phthalo Turquoise + Winsor Green + a bit of Titanium White.
Purple center: Narrow band of Ivory Black around side, away from feather shaft. Paint rest of area with Winsor Violet. Blend between.

2. Highlight as indicated, using chisel edge of a #2 or #4 bright, making narrow, close-together lines, indicating feather texture and growth direction.
Green band: Sap Green + Cadmium Yellow Pale + Winsor Green + Titanium White.
Rusty band: Accent in widest part with a little Winsor Violet. Highlight with Raw Sienna + Titanium White.
Turquoise band: Turquoise band mix (see above) + Titanium White.
Purple center: Purple band mix (see above) + Titanium White.

Tail

Note: Base shaft lines at bottom of tail with Titanium White.

1. Base area surrounding eyespots and the white shaft lines with Sap Green + Ivory Black.
2. Add the dozens of barb lines, alternately using the following mixes.
Mix 1: Phthalo Turquoise + Sap Green + Raw Sienna + Titanium White
Mix 2: Phthalo Turquoise + French Ultramarine + Raw Sienna + Titanium White
Frequently thin paint with odorless thinner. Follow growth direction of barbs carefully. Use photos as reference for color choice and direction of feathering.

Painted panel

Blossoms

1. Base with a slightly thinned mix of Titanium White + odorless thinner, using a small bright. Establish correct growth direction for individual petals with each stroke.

2. Shade with Oxide of Chromium + Ivory Black. Highlight with Titanium White, again with growth. Stipple in a center patch of fuzzy paint with Raw Umber + Burnt Sienna.

Stamens

See step 2 of Blossoms. Base stem of stamen with Burnt Sienna or Burnt Sienna + a touch of Winsor Red. Stipple stamen tips with the round brush and Cadmium Yellow Pale + Titanium White.

Single Feather Panel

Use the same painting instructions and palette as for the Peacock Feather Plate. Thin the paint as instructed for working on fabric with oils.

Painted panel

Rhododendrons
Green leaves

1. Base: Ivory Black + Sap Green.

2. Highlight: dirty brush + Oxide of Chromium + Titanium White. Add Burnt Sienna blemishes. Accent a few leaves behind peafowl's back with Raw Sienna. Paint a few white blemishes with Titanium White + Raw Sienna. Outline with Raw Umber.

Rusty brown leaves and stems

1. Base: Burnt Sienna.

2. Highlight: Raw Sienna + Titanium White.

Branches

1. Dark: Raw Umber. Light: Titanium White.

2. Blend slightly with chisel for branch-like texture.

Indian Peafowl Worksheet 1

Indian Peafowl Worksheet 2

Quilting
Quilt designed and quilted
by **Cindy Gensamer;**
pieced by **Cheri Blocker**

Skill level: Beginner/Intermediate
Finished wall hanging size: 26½" x 37½"

Materials

Note: Yardage is based on 42" wide useable fabric.
- Painted peafowl panel trimmed to 17½" x 28½"
- Painted feather panel trimmed to 7" x 12"
- ¼ yard *each* of nine assorted blue batik fabrics
- ¾ yards black tonal fabric (includes binding)
- 32" x 43" piece of backing fabric
- 32" x 43" piece of batting
- Thread in colors to match fabrics
- Basic sewing and rotary cutting supplies

Cutting

From each of the assorted blue batiks, cut:
One 2½" x 42" strip; recut each strip into three each of 3", 2½", 2", and 1" lengths

From the black tonal, cut:
Five 2½" x 42" strips; set aside four strips for the binding; recut the remaining strip into three each of 3", 2½", 2", and 1" lengths
Three 2" x 42" strips; recut into two 2" x 28½" strips and two 2" x 20½" strips

Directions

Note: Use a ¼" seam allowance throughout. Sew all pieces with right sides together and raw edges even, using matching thread.

Batik units. Following **Diagram 1** sew together one each of a 3", 2½", 2", and 1" batik piece. Using the photo as a guide and noting fabric placement, repeat to make a total of twenty-three 2½" x 7" units.

Do not press. (There will be some batik pieces left over.)

Diagram 1

Assembly

Note: Refer to the **Quilt Layout Diagram** for steps 1 through 4.

1. Sew one 2" x 28½" black strip to each long side of the peafowl panel. Stitch one 2" x 20½" black strip to the top of the panel and another to the bottom. Press seams toward the black fabric.

2. Noting color placement, lay ten batik units side by side. Press seams in every other unit in opposing directions; then matching seams, sew the units together. Noting orientation, stitch to the bottom of the peafowl panel.

3. In the same manner, position, press, then sew thirteen batik units together to make one long vertical strip. Stitch this pieced strip to the top of the feather panel.

4. Sew the feather section to the left side of the peafowl panel section.

5. Layer the quilt top right side up on top of the batting and the wrong side of the backing. Baste the layers together and quilt as desired. Trim the backing and batting even with the quilt top.

6. Bind using the four 2½" black strips. (See *General Quilting Directions*.)

Quilt Layout Diagram

Peafowl Feather Plate

Indian Peafowl Wall Hanging Companion Piece

Technique

Tips for wet-on-wet acrylic background. Thin all paint slightly with water. Before applying the second basecoat, drizzle a teaspoon, or so, of retarder directly on the surface. The retarder will mix in as the second coat is applied, and keep the surface workable while other colors are added.

Preparation

1. Seal and sand the wood.

2. Basecoat with a sponge roller and Quaker Grey. Let dry; sand, and wipe to remove dust.

3. Using same sponge roller, base with Cactus Green. Squeeze a little Blue Lagoon on one side of the surface. Blend softly into the background, then move a bit of the blue to the other side to

balance the color. Repeat process, using a little Woodland Night Green on the other side. Blend. Make soft gradations between colors, without overworking.

4. When dry, spray with sealer. Dry well.

5. Trace pattern from Pattern Section and transfer design to painting surface. Lay graphite paper on surface and arrange inked design on top of graphite. Lay a piece of tracing paper on top of design to protect original during transfer. Tape stack into position. Transfer design details completely and carefully using a ballpoint pen.

Painting

Feather barbs and shaft

1. Paint individual barb lines with slightly thinned Burnt Sienna + Raw Umber using a #4 bright. Use this mix for outlines of feather shaft.

2. Add feathery edges to barbs not attached to the eye with thinned Raw Sienna + Raw Umber and a round brush. Highlight down center of shaft with Titanium White + a touch of Raw Umber.

Eye of feathers

1. Base eye of each feather with the following color mixes:

Green band: Sap Green + Ivory Black + Winsor Green.

Rusty band: Narrow band of Raw Umber inside rusty band, next to finished green band. Paint remaining area with Burnt Sienna + Raw Sienna.

Turquoise band: Phthalo Turquoise + Winsor Green + touch Titanium White.

Purple center: Narrow band of Ivory Black around side away from feather shaft. Fill rest of area with Winsor Violet. Blend between.

2. Highlight as indicated, using chisel edge of a #2 or #4 bright. Make narrow, close-together lines, indicating feather texture and direction of growth.

Green band: Sap Green + Cadmium Yellow Pale + Winsor Green + Titanium White. Shade outside narrow green band with Raw Umber (dotted line on pattern).

Rusty band: Accent in widest part with a little Winsor Violet. Highlight with Raw Sienna + Titanium White.

Turquoise band: Turquoise band mix + Titanium White.

Purple center: Purple center mix (see above) + Titanium White.

Iridescence: Paint with a slightly thinned mix of Winsor Green + Sap Green + Cadmium Yellow Pale + Titanium White, and the point of the round rush. Add tiny rows of dots along feather barbs with a value dark enough to show up against background, and light enough to contrast with barb basecoat mix.

Highlight about ⅓" of each barb outside the outer band of Raw Umber shading with a little bit of Phthalo Turquoise + Titanium White. If too strong, tap with paper towel or fingertip, softening into the basecoat.

Finishing

1. Allow painting to dry for two weeks if you used Cobalt Drier; a month if not. When it is dry to the touch, clean up any remaining graphite lines with thinner. Wipe the piece with a damp cloth to remove any dust or thinner haze. Let dry thoroughly.

2. Spray with DecoArt Americana Acrylic Sealer/Finisher; wait an hour, and spray a second time.

Halloween Queen & Her Court Quilt

Bobbie Takashima

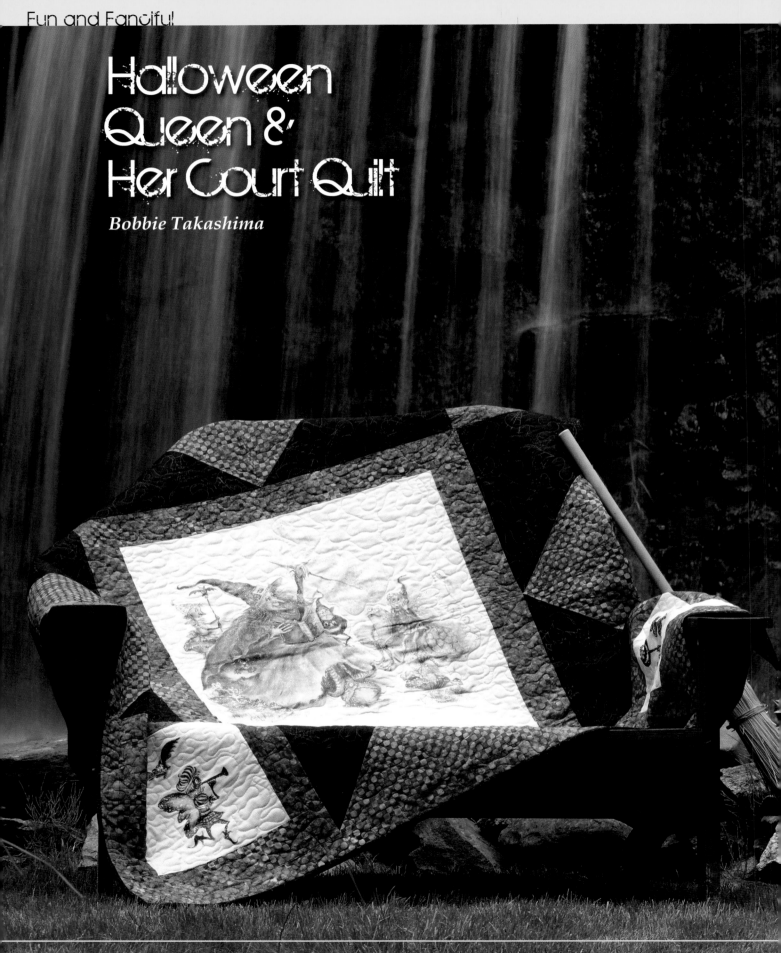

Create a shimmering masterpiece of magic and mystery!

Materials

- 1⅛ yards of cream crackle fabric
- *Chroma, Inc.* Jo Sonja's Artists' Colours: Aqua, Brilliant Green, Carbon Black, Dioxazine Purple, Indian Yellow, Napthol Crimson, Purple Madder, Titanium White, Transparent Magenta, Vermilion, Yellow Light
- *Jo Sonja's* Sure Touch Golden Taklon ½" angle (Series 1345), #2 round (Series 1350); #4 oval dry brush (Series 2010)
- *Chroma, Inc.* Jo Sonja's Textile Medium, Jo Sonja's Opal Dust
- *Miscellaneous:* tracing paper, gray transfer paper, pencil, waxed-paper palette

Preparation

1. Wash, dry, and iron fabric with no fabric softener, dryer sheets, or spray starch.

2. From the cream crackle fabric, cut one 25½" square and four 11½" squares.

3. Trace pattern from Pattern Section and lightly transfer onto fabric squares using gray transfer paper.

Painting

Note: Refer to the Worksheets on page 97 as you paint.

Center block brush sketching

1. Define the pattern and give the design a more painterly appearance by brush sketching Purple Madder + Textile Medium over the pattern lines. Use a waxed-paper palette for mixing and a brush that best fits each area.

2. Create a three-dimensional effect by shading along the pattern lines. With the same brush and mix from step 1, begin developing the shadows and the forms. Create soft edges using short, choppy strokes, increasing pressure on the brush where you want more color and decreasing pressure where you want less color. Stroke the brush toward the center of a rounded area, leaving the fabric background as the light value. Highlights will be painted on the lighter value fabric areas. This is an initial blocking in of the basic shapes.

3. Using the dirty brush, gradually deepen shading by brush mixing more Dioxazine Purple into the mix. Continue building shadows, working in smaller areas as the mix gets darker. Deepen the shadows and continue creating the roundness of the curved shapes.

4. As the design continues to take shape, add a touch of Carbon Black to the deepest, core-dark areas of the shape. Use this color to deepen the darkest shadows of the pattern. When the shading is finished, the design will have dimension. Allow the fabric to dry throughly before glazing.

Center block color washes

1. Apply the fun Halloween colors. Wash colors over the brush-sketched design, using thin layers of a mix of Textile Medium + a touch of water + pigment. Work the colors from the lightest and gradually move to the darker colors, getting smaller and darker.

2. Starting with a wash of Yellow Light, glaze over the main elements of the design. Add Indian Yellow to the shadow areas, staying out of the highlight areas. This should be very subtle coloring that gradually begins defining the shapes.

3. Starting in the shaded areas, wash over the orange elements of the design with Vermilion. Use this glaze on the mushrooms, pumpkins on the witch's cape, witch's hat and sleeves, and elves' clothes. Add touches of Vermilion here and there in the design.

4. Continue building the reds in the design with washes of Napthol Crimson. Deepen the shading in the red areas with Transparent Magenta.

5. Glaze over the green elements in the design with Brilliant Green.

6. Add the Aqua glaze to the underside of the mushrooms, the witch's hair, the elves, and in the shadows of the toads.

7. Wash a final glaze of Dioxazine Purple over the witch's skirt and cape and under the mushrooms. Add touches of Dioxazine Purple to the darkest areas of the design.

Center block details

1. Load the #2 round with a mix of Purple Madder + Carbon Black, and detail the facial features, bat on the stick, black cat, and witch's fingernails. Reinforce the darks in the witch's hair and anywhere details need to be defined.

2. Paint the white details, highlight lines, and dots with a brush mix of Titanium White + a touch of Yellow Light. These areas include the whiskers on the cat, dots and lines under the mushrooms, dots on the toads, and anywhere you need a little touch of light. Let dry.

Painted panel

Painted panel

Painted panel

Painted panel

Corner blocks

1. Paint each corner design with a brush mix of Carbon Black + Textile Medium. With the #4 oval dry brush or the #2 round, paint over the pattern lines using short, choppy strokes. Once the design is brush-sketched on, stroke along the shape of the dark areas. Allow the fabric color and light values to show through the design. These are the highlight areas of the design. Let dry.

2. Glaze each design with varying mixes of Titanium White + Vermilion and/or Yellow Light + Textile Medium. Using the #2 round, casually dab dots of any of the highlight mixes for detail interest on dark and light value areas of the design. Let dry.

Finishing

1. Brush on Opal Dust to add some sparkle to the design.

2. When the panels are dry, heat-set using the iron on the cotton setting. Place a piece of clean tracing paper over the top of the panel and iron for about 15 seconds. Remove tracing paper and iron again. Flip the fabric over and iron the back.

Painted panel

Halloween Queen & Her Court Worksheets

Quilting
Quilt designed, pieced, and quilted
by Cindy Gensamer

Skill level: Beginner/Intermediate
Center block size: 30" x 30"
Finished quilt size: 64" x 64"

Materials

Note: Yardage is based on 42" wide useable fabric.
- One painted witch panel trimmed to 24½" x 24½"
- Four painted corner panels trimmed to 10½" x 10½"
- 1 yard purple batik
- 1½ yards brown batik
- 1½ yards black spiderweb print (includes binding)
- 72" x 72" piece of backing fabric
- 72" x 72" piece of batting
- Thread in colors to match fabrics
- Basic sewing and rotary cutting supplies

Cutting

From the purple batik, cut:
Two 15⅞" x 42" strips; recut into four 15⅞" squares, then cut diagonally in half

From the brown batik, cut:
Four 3½" x 42" strips; recut into two 3½" x 24½" and two 3½" x 30½" pieces
Six 3" x 42" strips; recut into eight 3" x 15½" and eight 3" x 10½" pieces
Seven 2½" x 42" strips (for border)

From the black spiderweb print, cut:
Two 15⅞" x 42" strips; recut into four 15⅞" squares, then cut diagonally in half
Seven 2½" x 42" strips (for binding)

Assembly

Note: Use a ½" seam allowance throughout. Sew all pieces with right sides together and raw edges even, using matching thread. Press the seams toward the darker fabric unless otherwise indicated.

1. *Center panel.* Referring to **Diagram 1**, sew one 3½" x 24½" brown batik piece to each of two opposite sides of the painted witch panel. Stitch a 3½" x 30½" brown batik piece to the top of the panel and another to the bottom. Press the seams toward the brown fabric.

Diagram 1

2. *Side sections.* Sew a 15⅞" purple batik triangle to a 15⅞" black batik triangle as shown in **Diagram 2**. Make a total of eight 15½" squares. Noting orientation, stitch the squares together in pairs to make four sections.

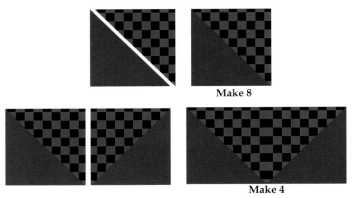

Make 8

Make 4

Diagram 2

3. *Corner units.* Following **Diagram 3**, sew one 3" x 10½" brown batik piece to each of two opposite sides of one painted corner panel. Stitch a 3" x 15½" brown batik piece to the top and another to the bottom. Press all seams toward the brown fabric. Repeat to make a total of four units.

Diagram 3

Make 4

4. Referring to the **Quilt Layout Diagram** and noting orientation, sew a side section to each of two opposite sides of the center panel. Press the seams toward the side sections. Stitch a corner unit to each end of the remaining two side sections and press seams toward the side units. Sew to the top and bottom of the center panel to complete the 60½″ x 60½″ quilt center.

5. *Border.* Stitch the seven 2½″ x 42″ brown batik strips short ends together to make a long strip. Cut two 64½″ lengths and two 60½″ lengths. Sew the shorter strips to the sides of the quilt center and the longer strips to the top and bottom. Press all the seams toward the brown fabric.

6. Layer the quilt top right side up on top of the batting and the wrong side of the backing. Baste the layers together and quilt as desired. Trim the backing and batting even with the quilt top.

7. Bind using the seven 2½″ black strips. (See *General Quilting Directions*.)

Quilt Layout Diagram

Round Halloween Box

Halloween Queen & Her Court Quilt Companion Piece

Materials

- *Turn of the Century Wood Products* Box (www.turnofthecentury-in.com)
- *Bear With Us, Inc*. Medium Round Finial, four for feet (#1795) and Witch Turning (www.bearwithusinc.com)
- *Chroma, Inc.* Jo Sonja's Artists' Colours: Aqua, Brilliant Green, Carbon Black, Dioxazine Purple, Indian Yellow, Napthol Crimson, Purple Madder, Titanium White, Transparent Magenta, Vermilion, Yellow Light
- *Jo Sonja's* Sure Touch Golden Taklon ½" angle (Series 1345), #2 round (Series 1350); #4 oval dry brush (Series 2010)
- *Chroma, Inc.* Jo Sonja's Clear Glaze Medium; Jo Sonja's Opal Dust; Jo Sonja's Satin Varnish (polyurethane)

Miscellaneous: tracing paper, gray transfer paper, sandpaper, wood glue

Preparation

1. Sand and wipe surfaces, if needed.

2. Glue the feet and knob on the box with wood glue, and let dry completely.

3. Basecoat the box with a mix of Vermilion + Clear Glaze Medium. When dry, sand and apply a second coat.

4. Drybrush some dark abstract patches on the box with a brush mix of Purple Madder + a little Vermilion. Wipe the brush and lighten the dirty brush with Yellow Light. Drybrush randomly around the box. Repeat, using the dirty brush and Indian Yellow. If desired, add touches of Titanium White to the mixes. The Purple Madder in the mix tones the colors. Let surface dry completely.

5. Trace the pattern from the Pattern Section and transfer the design.

Painting

Silhouette designs

1. Paint the design as described for the fabric, but do not use the Textile Medium. Paint each design with Carbon Black. With the #4 oval dry brush or the #2 round, paint over the pattern lines using short, choppy strokes. Once the design is brush-sketched on, stroke along the shape of the dark areas. Allow the background to show through the design. These are the highlight areas of the design. Let dry.

2. Glaze each design with mixes of Titanium White + Vermilion and/or Yellow Light. Using the #2 round, casually dab dots of any of the highlight mixes for detail interest on dark and light value areas of the design. Let dry.

Witch, pumpkins, and pumpkin trim

Use the same color progressions as described for the fabric, but do not mix with Textile Medium.

Finishing

1. Casually brush on Opal Dust over the entire box to add sparkle to the design.

2. When dry, apply several coats of satin varnish, allowing adequate drying time between each application.

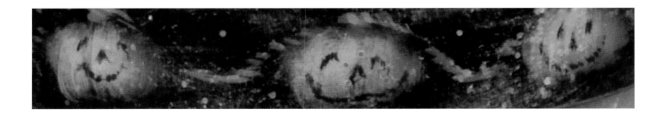

Fun and Fanciful

Hide-and-Seek Baby Quilt

Peggy Harris

Create a fun illusion of baby jack rabbits hiding in the tall grass!

Materials

- 1¼ yards grass print fabric
- *Plaid* FolkArt Fabric Paint (Brush On): Asphaltum, Engine Red, Fawn, Licorice, Light Red Oxide, Wicker White.
- *Silver Brush, Ltd.* Ruby Satin ⅛" and ¼" filbert grass comb (Series 2528S), #4 bright (Series 2502S), ⅜" angular (Series 2506S); Ultra Mini #12/0 angular (Series 2406S), #2 designer round (Series 2431S), #12/0 round (Series 2400S)
- *Miscellaneous:* flat surface (to secure fabric for painting), gray transfer paper, masking tape, mechanical pencil, stylus, tracing paper

Preparation

1. Launder, dry, and iron the fabric. Do not use fabric softener or starch.

2. Stretch and secure the fabric to a flat surface with masking tape.

3. Trace the rabbit and butterfly designs from the Pattern Section with the mechanical pencil. In any number and configuration desired, arrange rabbit and butterfly tracings on the fabric. Be sure to leave enough border fabric for the quilting process. For variety, some rabbit and butterfly patterns may be reversed.

4. Transfer the designs with gray transfer paper and the stylus. Do not transfer the butterfly wing veins at this time.

Painting

Note: At times, it may be helpful to dilute the paint with a small amount of water to aid spreading, but not so much as to dilute the color level of the paint.

Refer to the Worksheets on page 105 as you paint.

Rabbits

1. Mark the tip of the nose with Asphaltum and the #12/0 round brush. Load the #12/0 angular with Licorice and base the eye. When dry, overpaint the iris with Light Red Oxide. With the #12/0 round, establish the eyelid and drop a sparkling Wicker White highlight onto the eye. Add pink to the inner area of the ear with the #12/0 angular brush and a brush mix of Wicker White + Engine Red (8:1). When dry, shade the inner ear with Fawn and Asphaltum.

2. Using filbert combs (or the chisel of the bright brush), establish all areas of white fur, including the muzzle, inner ear, toe, and eye-surround fur. Use the comb brush flat or on its side with a chopping motion. Refer to the fur direction arrows on the pattern.

3. Establish all darkest areas of the fur with filbert combs of the appropriate size and Asphaltum. Refer to the fur direction arrows on the pattern for guidance. Add mid value fur with Fawn, blending into the darker and lighter fur areas as you work.

4. Enhance the fur with filbert combs and more color. Perfect individual hairs with the #2 designer round or the #12/0 round. Reinforce deepest shadows with touches of Licorice. Retouch, totally repaint, or create new blades of grass overlapping each rabbit. Match existing grass blades, or create new grass blade colors, with brush-mixed Fawn + Wicker White.

Butterflies

1. Underpaint the butterfly wings with the ⅜" angular brush and Wicker White. Undercoat the butterfly bodies with the #12/0 angular brush and Fawn.

2. Freehand (or lightly transfer and then paint) the antennae and wing veins with the #2 designer round brush and Asphaltum thinned with water. Clean up and perfect vein lines with the chisel edge of the clean, damp bright brush.

3. Shade the body with Asphaltum, and accent with Licorice. Add Licorice eyes and antennae knobs with the #12/0 round brush.

4. Paint the wing patterns with the #12/0 angular or the #12/0 round brush and Asphaltum. Float Fawn or Asphaltum shading as seen in the photos with the ⅜" angular brush.

Finishing

1. Air-dry the painting for 24 hours.

2. Heat-set with a dry iron using a pressing cloth. Painting may be hand- or machine-washed on cool after 72 hours.

3. Construct and quilt the fabric painting as shown.

Painted panel

Painted panel

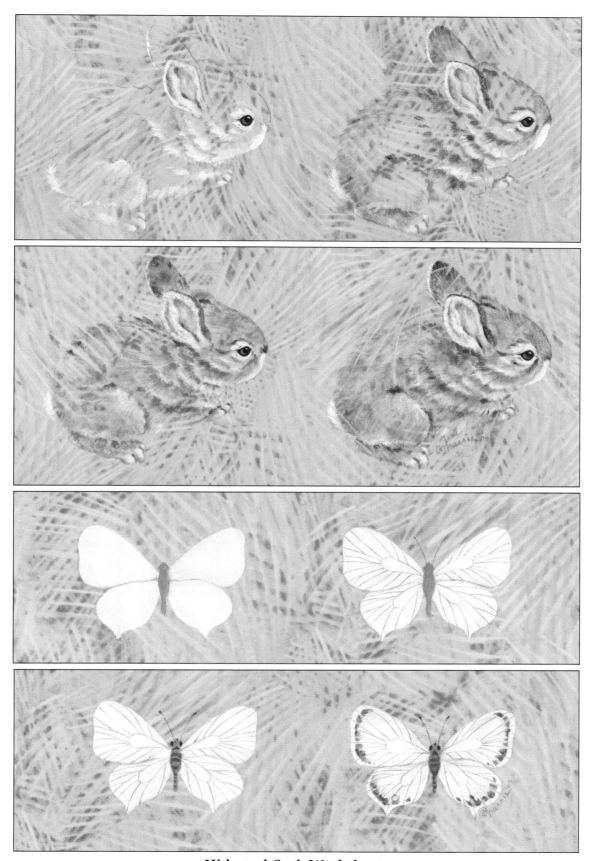

Hide-and-Seek Worksheets

Quilting
Quilted by Cindy Gensamer

Skill level: Beginner
Finished quilt size: 42" x 42"

Materials

Note: Yardage is based on 42" wide useable fabric.
- Painted quilt top trimmed to 40½" x 40½"
- ½ yard grass print fabric (same fabric that was used in the quilt top)
- 53" x 53" piece of batting
- 53" x 53" piece of backing fabric
- 5 yards of ecru cotton lace
- Thread in a color to match the fabric
- White wool for tails
- Fabric glue
- Basic sewing and rotary cutting supplies

Cutting

From the grass print, cut:
Five 2½" x 42" strips (for binding)

Assembly

Note: Refer to the quilt photo for steps 1 through 4.

1. Layer the painted quilt top right side up on top of the batting and wrong side of the backing. Baste the layers together and quilt as desired. (*Note:* This quilt was quilted by outlining the painted bunnies and butterflies.) Trim the backing and batting even with the quilt top.

2. Bind using the five 2½" x 42" grass print strips. (See *General Quilting Directions.*)

3. Hand-stitch the lace to the binding around all four sides.

4. Attach a small amount of white wool over each bunny's tail.

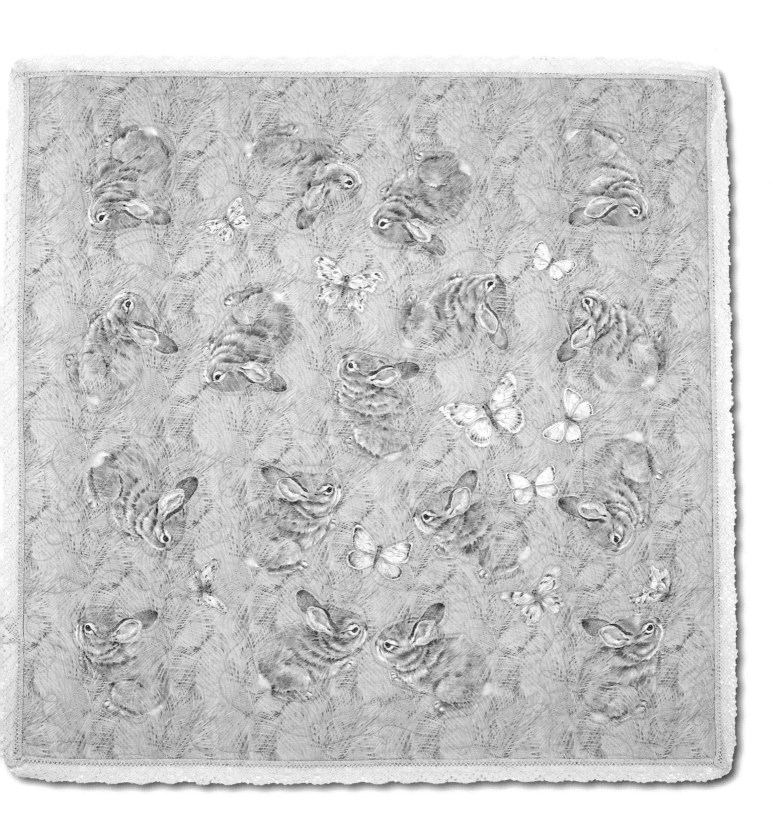

Door Plaque

Hide-and-Seek Baby Quilt Companion Piece

Materials

- *Western Metal Ware* Primed Metal Door Plaque (www.westernmetalware.com)
- *Plaid* FolkArt Artists' Pigments: Burnt Umber, Fawn, Light Red Oxide, Pure Black, Red Light, Titanium White, Warm White
- *Silver Brush, Ltd.* Ruby Satin ⅛" and ¼" filbert grass comb (Series 2528S), #4 bright (Series 2502S), ⅜" angular (Series 2506S); Ultra Mini #12/0 angular (Series 2406S), #2 designer round (Series 2431S), #12/0 round (Series 2400S); Golden Natural ¾" square wash (Series 2008S)
- *J.W. etc.* Right-Step Clear Varnish
- *Plaid* FolkArt Blending Gel Medium
- *Miscellaneous supplies:* gray transfer paper, hair dryer, mechanical pencil, stylus, tracing paper

Preparation

1. Base the plaque using the square wash brush with Warm White. Apply several coats, allowing adequate drying time between applications.

2. Trace the pattern from the Pattern Section for the rabbit and butterfly design with the mechanical pencil. Transfer the design with gray transfer paper and the stylus. Do not transfer the butterfly wing veins at this time.

Painting

Rabbits

1. Mark the tip of the nose with Burnt Umber and the #12/0 round brush. Base the eye with the #12/0 angular brush and Pure Black. When dry, overpaint the iris with Light Red Oxide. With the #12/0 round, establish the eyelid and drop a sparkling Titanium White highlight onto the eye. Add a pink brush mix of Titanium White + Red Light to the inner area of the ear with the #12/0 angular brush. When dry, shade the inner ear with Fawn and Burnt Umber.

2. Using Titanium White and the filbert combs (or the chisel of the bright brush), establish all areas of white fur, including the muzzle, inner ear, toe, and eye-surround fur. Add touches of pink to the muzzle and toes with a mix of Titanium White + Red Light (8:1). Refer to the fur direction arrows on the pattern.

3. Spread a slick of blending gel over the rabbit. Establish all darkest areas of the fur with filbert combs of appropriate size and Burnt Umber. Refer to the fur direction arrows on the pattern for guidance. Add mid value fur with Fawn, blending into the darker and lighter fur areas as you work.

4. Enhance the fur with filbert combs and more layers of gel/color, force-drying the painting with a hair dryer between layers. Perfect individual hairs with the #2 designer round or the #12/0 round.

Butterfly

1. Undercoat the butterfly bodies with the #12/0 angular brush and Fawn.

2. Freehand (or lightly transfer and then paint) the antennae and the wing veins with the #2 designer round brush and Burnt Umber thinned with water. Clean up or perfect the vein lines with the chisel edge of a clean, damp bright brush.

3. Shade the body with Burnt Umber, and accent with Pure Black. Add Pure Black eyes and antennae knobs with the #12/0 round brush.

4. Create the wing patterns with the #12/0 angular or the #12/0 round brush and Asphaltum. Float Fawn or Burnt Umber shading as seen in the photos with the ⅜" angular brush.

Finishing

1. Carefully paint the lettering with the #2 designer round brush and a mix of Fawn + Warm White (2:1). The #12/0 angular may be helpful with thicker strokes of the letters. Freehand the short grasses around the rabbit feet with the same mix. Let dry.

2. Finish the plaque with several coats of varnish, allowing adequate drying time between each application.

For Fun Child's Quilt

Chris Thornton-Deason

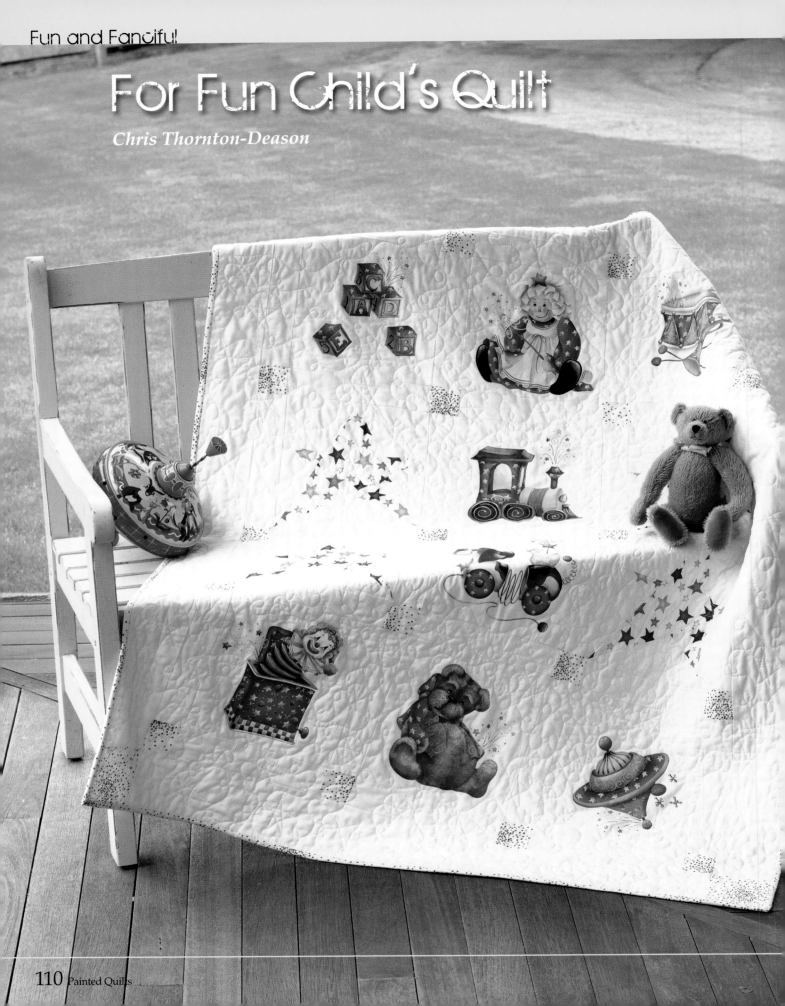

*A child's quilt painted and pieced with love will
become a treasured family heirloom!*

Materials

- 2⅓ yards of white tonal fabric (for 8 painted squares; reserve the remaining for quilting instructions)
- *DecoArt* Americana SoSoft Fabric Paint: Bittersweet Orange, Brown, Buttermilk, Cadmium Orange, Cadmium Yellow, Christmas Red, Hauser Dark Green, Lamp Black, Mediterranean Blue, Ocean Blue, True Green, Wine, Ultra White
- *DecoArt* Americana SoSoft Fabric Paint (Neons): Neon Red, Neon Yellow
- *DecoArt* SoSoft Glitters: Glimmer
- *Royal & Langnickel* White Taklon #6, #8, #10, and #12 shader (Series R-159); White Taklon #1 script liner (Series R-589), ½" Wisp Brush (Series #R2735)
- *DecoArt* Laurie Speltz's Instant Images Stencils: Backgrounds (#IIJ05) and Celebration (#IIP06); Laurie Speltz's ¼" Duo Tool
- *Miscellaneous supplies:* artist's tape, circle template, paper towels, pencil, scissors, small ½" flower stencil of choice, tracing paper, transfer paper

Preparation

1. Wash, dry, and iron the fabric. Do not use fabric softener, dryer sheets, or spray starch. From the white fabric, cut eight 12" squares.

2. Trace patterns from Pattern Section and transfer basic pattern lines to each white fabric square.

3. Using the #12 shader, paint an even basecoat of Ultra White over entire toy on each block. This will help make primary colors appear brighter. Let dry.

4. Transfer pattern details to each block.

Techniques

- Take care to stay in the lines of the patterns. Primary colors are somewhat transparent and do not cover each other well.
- Basecoat and shading steps are completed using a wet-on-wet technique. While the basecoat is still wet, work shadows into the basecoat color. Start by laying shadow color on the line, working into the center of any given area. Base paint, shade, and float highlights using an appropriate-sized brush for the area in which you are working.
- *Stenciling technique.* Hold the stencil firmly in place. Pick up a small amount of color with the ¼" Duo Tool, and pat on palette to remove any excess paint. Use a straight up-and-down motion to pat over the desired areas of the stencil. Repeat randomly as many times as desired. *Tip:* Applying two thin coats is preferable, as it prevents bleeding.
- *All blocks.* On the red areas of each toy, double-load the Duo Tool with Bittersweet Orange and Cadmium Yellow, and randomly stencil the small star from the Background Stencil.

Painting

Note: Refer to the Worksheets on pages 115–118 for each block to see the progression of shading, highlighting, and detailing.

Wooden blocks

1. *Basecoat and shade.* Base front and sides of blocks with Buttermilk + a tiny touch of Brown; shade with Dark Chocolate + a touch of Lamp Black. Base tops of blocks Christmas Red; shade with Wine. Base front borders of each alphabet block and letters with colors of choice; shade with the appropriate colors.

2. *Highlight.* Highlight front and sides of blocks with Ultra White, and tops with Neon Red.

3. *Detail.* Highlight letters and faces of blocks with Ultra White + a touch of basecoat color. Load the script liner with coordinating dark color, and outline letters and the inside border of blocks. Line numbers on sides with Lamp Black.

Doll

1. *Basecoat and shade.* Base apron with Buttermilk + a tiny touch of Brown; shade with Dark Chocolate + a touch of Lamp Black. Base dress Christmas Red; shade with Wine. Base hair with Cadmium Yellow; shade

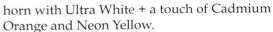

with Bittersweet Orange. Base star in doll's hair with True Green + a touch of Ultra White; shade with Hauser Dark Green. Base face with Ultra White + a touch of Brown; shade lightly with Brown. Base shoes Lamp Black.

2. *Highlight.* Highlight apron with Ultra White, dress with Neon Red, and hair with Neon Yellow. Highlight star in hair with Ultra White + a touch of True Green and Neon Yellow, and shoes with Ultra White + a touch of Lamp Black and Ocean Blue.

3. *Detail.* Lightly float cheeks with the #10 shader and Christmas Red + a touch of Ultra White. Paint nose same color with liner. Line eyes, eyelashes, and mouth with Lamp Black. Line apron with Ocean Blue; shade with Mediterranean Blue. Line Ocean Blue stitching on apron. Line wand with Ultra White + a touch of Brown; shade with Brown. Float highlight on shoes and eyes with Ultra White + a touch of Ocean Blue. Add sparkle highlights to facial features, wand, star, and shoes with Ultra White.

Drum and horn

1. *Basecoat and shade.* Base drumstick handles with Brown + a touch of Buttermilk and Bittersweet Orange; shade with Brown. Base skin of drum with Buttermilk + a tiny touch of Brown; shade with Dark Chocolate + a touch of Lamp Black. Base red triangles and balls at ends of drumsticks Christmas Red; shade with Wine. Base blue triangles Ocean Blue; shade with Mediterranean Blue. Base top and bottom rim with Cadmium Yellow; shade with Bittersweet Orange. Base horn Cadmium Orange; shade with Bittersweet Orange.

2. *Highlight.* Highlight handles with Buttermilk + a touch of Brown and Bittersweet Orange. Highlight skin of drum with Ultra White. Highlight red triangles and drumstick balls with Neon Red, and blue triangles with Ultra White + a touch of Ocean Blue. Highlight top and bottom rim of drum with Neon Yellow. Highlight

horn with Ultra White + a touch of Cadmium Orange and Neon Yellow.

3. *Detail.* Load script liner with Ultra White + a touch of Cadmium Yellow, and paint small swirls on blue areas. Double-load the Duo Tool with True Green + a touch of Ultra White and Hauser Dark Green. Stencil the medium star from the Celebration Stencil on horn. Stencil the swirls below horn star with Ultra White + a touch of Cadmium Yellow. Randomly line swirls with Neon Yellow and Bittersweet Orange. Paint dots and lacing on drum with True Green + a touch of Ultra White; shade with Hauser Dark Green. Apply sparkle highlights on the lacing, knobs, swirls, and bottom and top rim with the script liner and Ultra White.

Train

1. *Basecoat and shade.* Base roof with Brown + a touch of Buttermilk and Bittersweet Orange; shade with Brown. Base cab and smokestack Christmas Red; shade with Wine. Base boiler and inside of windows Cadmium Yellow; shade with Bittersweet Orange. Base the stripe in the center of train and headlight with True Green + a touch of Ultra White; shade with Hauser Dark Green. Base the cowcatcher and sign Ocean Blue; shade with Mediterranean Blue. Basecoat wheels with Lamp Black + Ultra White (1:1); shade with Lamp Black.

2. *Highlight.* Highlight train roof with Buttermilk + a touch of Brown and Bittersweet Orange. Highlight cab and smokestack with Neon Red. Highlight the round part of train and inside windows with Neon Yellow. Highlight stripe in center of train and headlight with Ultra White + a touch of True Green and Neon Yellow. Highlight cowcatcher and sign with Ultra White + a touch of Ocean Blue. Highlight wheels with Ultra White + a touch of Lamp Black and Ocean Blue.

3. *Detail.* Paint stripes on roof with the script liner and True Green + a touch of Ultra White. Shade stripe ends with Hauser Dark Green. Outline center green stripe and paint swirls on wheels with Ocean Blue; shade with Mediterranean Blue. Base engine emblem circle with Ocean Blue; shade with Mediterranean Blue. Load script liner with Neon Yellow + a

touch of True Green, and highlight green stripe on the roof. Paint band emblem and numbers with Cadmium Yellow + a touch of Ultra White. Using the script liner, highlight emblem letters with streaks of Ultra White. Highlight blue stripes and swirls with Ultra White + a touch of Ocean Blue. Highlight wheels with streaks of Ultra White.

Dog and duck

1. *Basecoat and shade.* Base dog's body Buttermilk + a tiny touch of Brown; shade with Dark Chocolate + a touch of Lamp Black. Base spots with Brown + a touch of Buttermilk and Bittersweet; shade with Brown. Base dog's back, ears, and nose Lamp Black. Base wheels and ball at end of tail Christmas Red; shade with Wine. Base duck with Cadmium Yellow; shade with Bittersweet Orange. Base star with Ocean Blue; shade with Mediterranean Blue.

2. *Highlight.* Highlight brown spots with Buttermilk + a touch of Brown and Bittersweet Orange. Highlight dog's body with Ultra White. Highlight wheels and tail ball with Neon Red, and duck and collar with Neon Yellow. Highlight star on stick with Ultra White + a touch of Ocean Blue. Highlight dog's back, ears, and nose with Ultra White + a touch of Lamp Black and Ocean Blue.

3. *Detail.* Line the stick holding the star with the script liner and True Green. Line pull string with Cadmium Orange, shade with Bittersweet Orange, highlight with Cadmium Orange + a touch of Ultra White. Base collar star and pull string ball with True Green + a touch of Ultra White; shade with Hauser Dark Green. Base eye with the script liner and Ultra White. Use same brush and Ultra White + a touch of Lamp Black to line springs, collar, and eye screw on dog's chest; shade with Lamp Black. Line eyes and paint pupil, mouth, dots on dog's muzzle, and dot duck's eye with Lamp Black. Base center of eye and center of wheels with Ocean Blue; shade with Mediterranean Blue. Paint duck's beak Cadmium Orange; highlight with Ultra White + a touch of Cadmium Orange. With the flower stencil, very lightly stencil Ultra White flowers on duck's back. Outline flowers with script liner and Cadmium Orange. Dot the center with the brush handle tip and Cadmium Orange. Paint all bright highlights on the stars, springs, knobs, ears, nose, and in duck's and dog's eyes with Ultra White.

Jack-in-the-box

1. *Basecoat and shade.* Base sides and lid Christmas Red; shade with Wine. Base collar, checked area, and top of box with Cadmium Yellow; shade with Bittersweet Orange. Base every other stripe on body with True Green + a touch of Ultra White; shade with Hauser Dark Green. Base every other ring on body, the knob, and the hat brim with Ocean Blue; shade with Mediterranean Blue. Base top of forehead with Ultra White + a touch of Brown; shade lightly with Brown. Base the bottom of face with Ultra White, working Ocean Blue across chin.

2. *Highlight.* Highlight sides and lid with Neon Red, and checkered area and the top of box with Neon Yellow. Highlight every other stripe on body with Ultra White + a touch of True green and Neon Yellow. Highlight the knob and stippling on hat brim and ball, and every other ring on body, with Ultra White + a touch of Ocean Blue.

3. *Detail.* Double-load the Duo Tool with Ocean Blue and Mediterranean Blue, and randomly stencil dots on side of box using the Background Stencil. Lightly float cheeks with the #10 shader and Christmas Red. Using script liner, apply facial features as follows: eyes with Ocean Blue; nose with Christmas Red, and shade with Wine; mouth with Cadmium Orange, and shade with Christmas Red; eyebrows with Brown. Double-load the #10 shader with Ocean Blue and Mediterranean Blue, and apply bottom row of checks, with dark at bottom. Paint upper row with a double-load of Ocean Blue + a touch of Ultra White, keeping light at top. Line mouth and eyes and add pupils with Lamp Black. Apply lines to collar with script liner and Ocean Blue. Highlight facial features with Ultra White. Highlight body sections with long Ultra White comma strokes. Paint Xs on sides of box with script liner and True Green + a touch of Ultra White. Apply small Ultra White dots on sides of the box with brush handle tip.

Bear

1. *Basecoat and shade.* Base bear with Brown + a touch of Buttermilk and Bittersweet Orange; shade with Brown. Base bow with Christmas Red; shade with Wine. Base vest with Ocean Blue; and shade with Mediterranean Blue.

2. *Highlight.* Create little short hairs using the ½" Wisp Brush with Buttermilk + a touch of Brown and Bittersweet Orange. Highlight bow with Neon Red, and vest with Ultra White + a touch of Ocean Blue.

3. *Detail.* Line small swirls on vest with Ultra White + a touch of Cadmium Yellow. Randomly line swirls with Neon Yellow and Bittersweet Orange. Line vest with True Green + a touch of Ultra White, and facial features with Lamp Black. Wash fur with touches of Bittersweet Orange and Cadmium Yellow. Highlight eyes and nose with Ocean Blue. Shade green vest trim Hauser Dark Green. Apply sparkle highlights to face with Ultra White.

Top

1. *Basecoat and shade.* Base sticks holding knobs with Brown + a touch of Buttermilk and Bittersweet Orange; shade with Brown. Base first ring with Cadmium Yellow; shade with Bittersweet Orange. Base second ring and both knobs with Ocean Blue; shade with Mediterranean Blue. Base third ring and ball with Christmas Red; shade with Wine. Base fourth ring with Cadmium Orange; shade with Bittersweet Orange. Base the bottom True Green + a touch of Ultra White; shade with Hauser Dark Green.

2. *Highlight.* Highlight sticks holding knobs with Buttermilk + a touch of Brown and Bittersweet Orange. Highlight first ring on top with Neon Yellow. Highlight second ring and both knobs with Ultra White + a touch of Ocean Blue. Highlight third ring and ball with Neon Red. Highlight fourth ring with Ultra White + a touch of Cadmium Orange and Neon Yellow. Highlight bottom with Ultra White + a touch of True Green.

3. *Detail.* Load the script liner with Ultra White + a touch of Cadmium Yellow, and paint small swirls on blue band. Double-load Duo Tool with Ocean Blue and Mediterranean Blue, and randomly stencil dots on the bottom of the top using Background Stencil. Line with Cadmium Orange + a touch of Ultra White. Stripe yellow area with True Green + a touch of Ultra White. Shade stripes with the script liner and Hauser Dark Green; highlight with Neon Yellow + a touch of True Green. Line jacks with Ultra White + a touch of Lamp Black; shade with Lamp Black. Randomly apply swirls using a script liner and Neon Yellow and Bittersweet Orange. Highlight jacks, blue bands, and knobs with Ultra White.

Finishing

1. Accent each block with star and swirl patterns from the Celebrations Stencil. Load the Duo Tool with Cadmium Yellow + a touch of Ultra White and Bittersweet Orange, and stencil swirls. Stencil stars using any colors from the palette.

2. Using the #10 shader, randomly dab Glitters on the highlighted areas and stenciled star and swirl accents.

For Fun Block Worksheet

For Fun Doll Worksheet

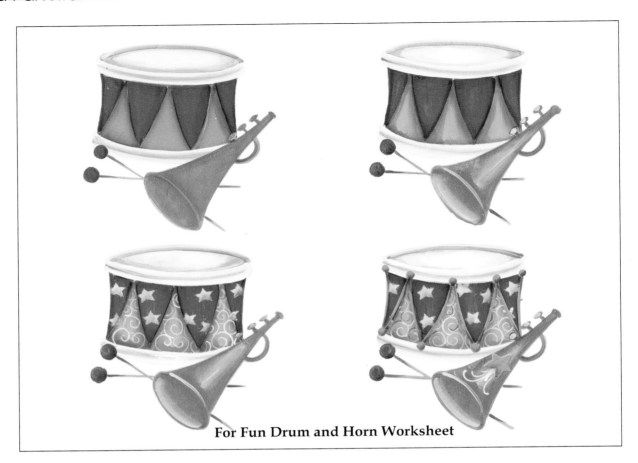

For Fun Drum and Horn Worksheet

For Fun Train Worksheet

For Fun Dog and Duck Worksheet

For Fun Jack-in-the-Box Worksheet

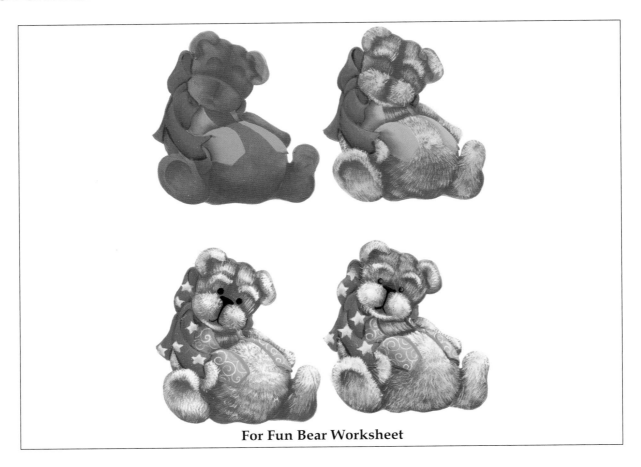

For Fun Bear Worksheet

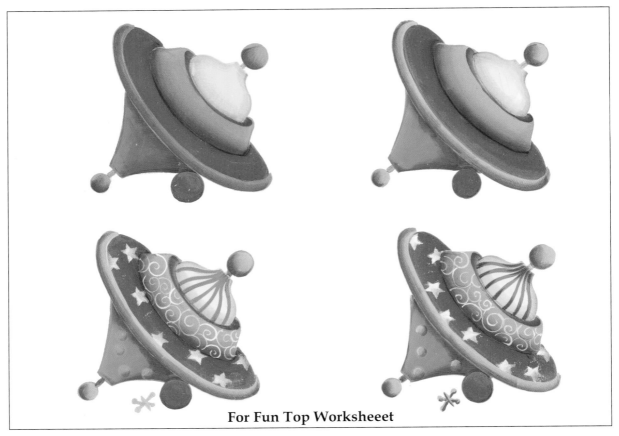

For Fun Top Worksheeet

Toy Box

For Fun Child's Quilt Companion Piece

Materials

- Toy box*
- *DecoArt* Americana Acrylics*; Burnt Orange (Bittersweet Orange), Light Cinnamon (Brown), Buttermilk (Buttermilk), Tangelo Orange (Cadmium Orange), Cadmium Yellow (Cadmium Yellow), Santa Red (Christmas Red), Hauser Dark Green (Hauser Dark Green), Lamp Black (Lamp Black), True Blue (Mediterranean Blue), Primary Red (Neon Red), Primary Yellow (Neon Yellow), Turquoise Blue (Ocean Blue), Kelly Green + a touch of Snow White (True Green), Snow White (Ultra White), Cranberry Wine (Wine)
- * *Parentheses indicate equivalent SoSoft Fabric Paint color used in quilt instructions.*
- *Royal & Langnickel* Aqualon #6, #8, #10, and #12 shader (Series 2150), #1 script liner (Series 2585), 1″ wash/glaze brush (Series 2700), ½″ Wisp Brush (Series #R2735)
- *DecoArt* DuraClear Satin Varnish; Star Lite Top Coat; Laurie Speltz's Instant Images Stencil: Backgrounds (#IIJ05) and Celebration (#IIP06); Laurie Speltz's ¼″ Duo Tool
- *Miscellaneous:* artist's tape, circle template, paper towels, pencil, sandpaper, small ½″ flower stencil of choice, soft cloth, tracing paper, transfer paper

Featured toy box purchased at Michael's Stores, Inc.

Preparation

1. Sand box and wipe to remove dust.
2. Base top of box and squares on sides of box with several coats of Snow White; bottom with Primary Yellow.
3. Use colors of choice to base letters on sides of box.
4. Trace and transfer pattern from Pattern Section to lid.

Painting

Paint the design on the lid following the instructions for the quilt, but substituting DecoArt Americana Acrylics for SoSoft Fabric Paints.

Finishing

1. Embellish the letters on sides of box with the stencil designs.
2. Apply several coats of satin varnish, allowing adequate drying time between applications.
3. When dry, apply Star Lite Top Coat to the letters on bottom of box and to swirls and stars on lid of box. Let dry.

Quilting

Quilt designed and quilted
by **Cindy Gensamer;**
pieced by **Gloria Ware**

Skill level: Beginner/Intermediate
Finished quilt size: 46" x 58"
Finished block size: 10" x 10"
Number of blocks: 8 Painted; 4 Star

Materials

Note: Yardage is based on 42" wide useable fabric.
- Eight painted toy blocks trimmed to 10½" x 10½"
- ⅔ yard of white fabric with multicolored stars
- ¾ yard of white fabric with polka dots
- ⅞ yard white-on-white print fabric
- Reserved white tonal fabric
- 54" x 54" piece of backing fabric
- 54" x 54" piece of batting
- Thread in colors to match fabrics
- Template plastic
- Basic sewing and rotary cutting supplies

Cutting

Note: Patterns for the star pieces, 1 through 9, are located in the pattern envelope and include the ¼" seam allowance. Trace pattern pieces onto template plastic, transfer grain line markings, and cut out neatly.

From the white with multicolored stars, cut:
Four each of pieces 2, 4, 6, and 8 with the arrows positioned on the straight of grain

From the white with polka dots, cut:
One 4½" x 42½" strip; recut into four 4½" squares and nine 2½" squares
Seven 2½" x 42" strips; recut one strip into eleven 2½" squares; reserve the remaining strips for the binding

From the white-on-white print, cut:
Ten 2½" x 42" strips; recut into thirty-one 2½" x 10½" pieces (for sashing)

From the white tonal fabric, cut:
Five 4½" x 42" strips; recut two strips into 4½" x 38½" strips (for border)
Four each of pieces 1, 3, 5, 7, and 9 with the arrows positioned on the straight of grain

Directions

Note: Use a ¼" seam allowance throughout. Sew all pieces with right sides together and raw edges even, using matching thread. Press seams toward the darker fabric unless otherwise indicated

Star blocks
1. Following **Diagram 1a**, sew piece 2 between pieces 1 and 3, then stitch piece 4 to the long side. Sew piece 5 to piece 6 as shown in **Diagram 1b**, and stitch piece 8 between pieces 7 and 9 as shown in **Diagram 1c**.
2. Referring to the **Block Diagrams**, sew the three sections together to complete the 10½" x 10½" block.
3. Repeat steps 1 and 2 to make a total of four blocks.

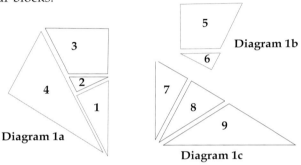

Diagram 1a   Diagram 1b   Diagram 1c

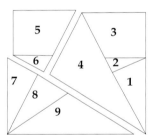   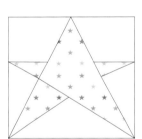

Block Diagrams   Make 4

Assembly

Note: Refer to the **Quilt Layout Diagram** for steps 1 through 4.
1. *Block rows.* Sew four 2½" x 10½" white-on-white print pieces alternately together with three toy blocks to make the top row. Press seams toward the sashing pieces. Noting placement, make three additional rows using the remaining toy blocks, star blocks, and sashing pieces.
2. *Sashing rows.* Stitch four 2½" polka-dot squares alternately together with three 2½" x 10½" sashing pieces. Press the seams toward the sashing pieces. Repeat to make a total of five rows.

3. Sew the sashing rows alternately together with the block rows (*Note:* The two-star block rows are sewn between the two-toy block rows) to complete the 38½" x 50½" quilt center.

4. Sew one 4½" x 38½" white tonal strip to the top of the quilt center and another to the bottom. Press seams toward the border strips. Stitch the remaining three white tonal strips short ends together to make one long strip. Cut two 50½"

lengths. Stitch a 4½" polka-dot square to each end of both strips, then sew to the sides of the quilt center.

5. Layer the quilt top right side up on top of the batting and the wrong side of the backing. Baste the layers together and quilt as desired. Trim the backing and batting even with the quilt top.

6. Bind using the six 2½" x 42" polka-dot strips. (See *General Quilting Directions.*)

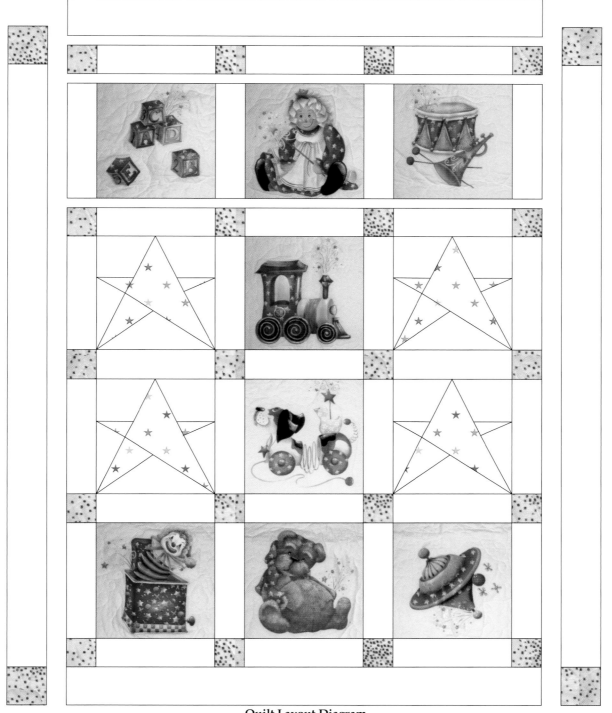

Quilt Layout Diagram

Acorn Cove Quilt

Cynthia Erekson

Rich heirloom print fabric combines with quaint autumn seacoast scenes for this fabulous New England quilt!

Materials

- 1⅞ yards of mustard tonal fabric (⅞ yard for painting; reserve remaining for quilting instructions)
- *DecoArt* Americana Acrylics: Antique Teal, Black Green, Bleached Sand, Cool Neutral, Lamp Black, Milk Chocolate, Raw Sienna, Tangerine, Traditional Burnt Sienna
- *Loew-Cornell* Fabric # 4 and #6 shader (Series 223), ¼" and ⅜" angular shader (Series 224), #2 liner Series 227), #1, #3, and #5 round scrubber (Series 228); Nylon Stencil ⅝" blender (Series 4412) (available as a set of 2)
- Brushes of choice: old scruffy flat, ½" soft stencil brush
- *Sakura* Pigma Micron Marker #05, Black
- *Miscellaneous:* index card, chalk pencil, compass*, craft knife*, fabric eraser, ten 13" freezer paper squares, ¼" masking tape, ½ yard muslin, palette knife, paper towels, ruler, sharp scissors or rotary cutter, small pane of glass*, stylus, tracing paper, transfer paper (gray and white)

*Optional

Preparation

1. Press unwashed fabric. (If you choose to wash the fabric, do not use fabric softener.) Cut two 14" x 42" strips; recut into five 14" squares, with attention to print direction since squares will be positioned "on point" (diamond shape) in the quilt.

Place the shiny side of a freezer paper square against the wrong side of a fabric square, and press with a dry, hot iron on the right side of the fabric. Turn the square over and quickly press with the paper side up until the fabric adheres. Repeat for all squares. Prepare a smaller freezer-papered scrap of fabric to use for practice painting.

2. Center and trace the outer design circles (or use a compass) onto the dull side of the remaining five freezer paper squares. Cut out circles with scissors, or a sharp craft knife on a pane of glass. Place each piece of freezer paper with a circle cutout onto the right side of the fabric squares, shiny side down, and press gently to adhere these "stencils" to the fabric.

3. Trace and number the patterns from the Pattern Section. Lightly transfer only the horizon line and the waterline onto each square. Number each square to correspond with the tracing. Make sure the fabric square is "on point" and the print direction is correct.

Techniques

- Scrub the colors for all sky and ground areas horizontally across the circle, using very little paint on the blender brush. Build up light layers of color for heavier coverage.
- When basecoating, use the shader, angular shader, and liner brushes that best suit the size of an area.
- When shading and highlighting, use various sizes of round scrubbers.
- When painting, the paintbrushes *must not* have any water in them. Be sure to dry them completely or have multiple brushes.

Painting

Note: Please read complete instructions before beginning the project. Practice painting first on the prepared scrap of fabric.

Refer to the Worksheet on page 126.

Scenes

1. *Sky.* Dip the blender brush into Antique Teal. Stroke the brush on the palette, flip, and repeat. Stroke the brush with a bit of pressure on a paper towel to remove excess paint. Flip and repeat. With the chisel edge of the brush, lightly scrub side to side to define the horizon line. Next, lay the brush on the freezer paper at one edge of the circle. Press the brush and pull the color horizontally across the sky area. Repeat from the opposite side of the circle. Begin with light pressure until you see how much color is deposited on the fabric. Scrub in color side to side in the middle area of the sky. Some print should be visible through the paint. Let dry and add another light coat, if needed. Scrub in some random darker cloudy areas.

2. *Water.* Repeat this technique for the water, using slightly more paint in the brush. The print remains visible through the water. Wash and dry the brush.

3. *Ground.* With the same brush, scrub Milk Chocolate across the ground area. Don't get too dark. Wipe all color out of brush on a paper towel. Reload with Tangerine and remove excess paint from the brush. Using the chisel edge, highlight the hilltop. Scrub in patches of Tangerine throughout the sky and the ground.

4. *Shading around scene.* Create subtle, soft shading around the edge of the circle with a #5 round scrubber. Dip the brush into Lamp Black, then scrub on a paper towel until almost no paint remains. Place the brush, with the bristles flat, half on the edge of the freezer

paper and half on the edge of the scene. Scrub lightly and smoothly all around the edge of the circle without lifting the brush (except to reload), increasing pressure as the brush dries out.

5. Repeat these background steps on all five fabric squares before proceeding. Once dry, transfer the remaining pattern lines onto the squares, excluding details.

6. *Buildings.* Basecoat all buildings, including roof shapes, with a shader, or angular shader, and Raw Sienna, Traditional Burnt Sienna, and Cool Neutral. When dry, paint around roof edges with Lamp Black and a small angular shader, dragging the color across the roof from the edges toward the center. Leave a highlight of the undercoat showing through the center of the roof. Paint foundation of the Cool Neutral building with Traditional Burnt Sienna.

Note: Shade and highlight all buildings by placing the straight edge of an index card along the edge to be painted. Use a very dry round scrubber brush, with most paint scrubbed off on a paper towel. Scrub up and down, with the bristles half on the paper and half on the building; then press the bristles onto the paper and pull the color horizontally across the building, lifting to achieve an uneven edge.

Highlight all buildings with Tangerine. Shade all buildings using a clean, dry brush and Lamp Black.

7. *Whales, boats, and pylons.* Paint whales, boats, and pylons Lamp Black. Highlight boats by lightly scrubbing with Tangerine.

8. *Trees.* Lightly base all trees Black Green. Shade by scrubbing with Lamp Black. Highlight with a drybrush of Tangerine. Line trunks with Lamp Black. Base sails with Cool Neutral. Highlight with a drybrush of Bleached Sand. Tea-stain sails by scrubbing small areas lightly with Tangerine.

9. Transfer details onto the scenes.

10. *Details.* Paint all birds with the liner and Cool Neutral. Lightly stroke Bleached Sand highlights on wings. With a liner and Lamp Black, paint wagon, wagon post, and whale weathervane. Highlight wagon with Tangerine. Paint wheels Traditional Burnt Sienna. Highlight with a stroke of Tangerine. Paint some of the pumpkins with Traditional Burnt Sienna, and others with a mixture of Traditional Burnt Sienna plus varying amounts of Tangerine. Highlight with Tangerine. Shade by lightly scrubbing with Lamp Black. Paint chimneys with Traditional Burnt Sienna. Thin Cool Neutral with a touch of water, and paint the smoke. Using the liner, paint signposts Lamp Black and signs Cool Neutral. Dab signs lightly with Lamp Black to shade. Add a small Traditional Burnt Sienna pumpkin to one sign. Highlight with a dab of Tangerine. Line pumpkin stems with Lamp Black.

11. *Man.* Paint the entire shape of the man lightly with Lamp Black. Paint hat brim with a liner and Lamp Black slightly thinned with water. Darken top part of the hat with Lamp Black. Create the face with Traditional Burnt Sienna + Cool Neutral. Dab on a touch of Traditional Burnt Sienna to suggest a cheek and nose tip. Paint jacket and shoes Traditional Burnt Sienna. Darken pants and hands with Lamp Black. Highlight jacket with Tangerine, and shade with Lamp Black. Thin Cool Neutral slightly with water, and add the collar and a small hatband.

12. *Shading.* Shade beneath all buildings, trees, signposts, and the wagon using Milk Chocolate on the chisel edge of the blender brush. First wipe on a paper towel, removing excess paint from the brush; then lightly scrub side to side to deposit subtle color. Add the paths and random shadows. Reload brush with Lamp Black, remove excess paint, and darken some of the Milk Chocolate shading and paths. Shade beneath whales, boats, pylons, and any birds in the water with Lamp Black. Use the tip of a well-loaded liner to dab distinct foam on the water. Remove freezer paper stencils from the fronts of the squares.

13. *Marker details.* Use the fine-point marker to add small details, seen on the pattern and in the photos, such as doors, fences, buttons, bird legs, wheel centers, and ropes.

14. *Ground accents.* Using an old scruffy flat brush, lightly pounce Antique Teal bushes throughout the ground. Practice on a scrap first.

15. Dot the top of one boat's mast using a brush handle and Tangerine.

Acorn and leaf border

Base all acorns Milk Chocolate with Lamp Black caps and stems. Highlight acorns and caps Tangerine, and shade acorns Lamp Black. Paint leaves with Traditional Burnt Sienna. Randomly scrub in some Antique Teal areas on each leaf. Highlight leaves with Tangerine, and shade with Lamp Black. Thin Milk Chocolate slightly and line leaf veins. Either paint border comma strokes with Lamp Black and a round brush, or cut stencils from freezer paper and scrub in color.

Finishing

1. Let squares dry thoroughly. Erase all visible transfer lines.

2. Heat-set the paint. Remove the freezer paper from fabric. Place a painted square face down on a piece of muslin. Fold over excess muslin to make a muslin sandwich with the painted fabric inside. Press the painted area with a hot, dry iron. Leave the iron in place until the fabric is very hot but not scorching. Pick up, rather than slide, the iron to heat another area. Flip the "sandwich" over and press until very hot on the second side.

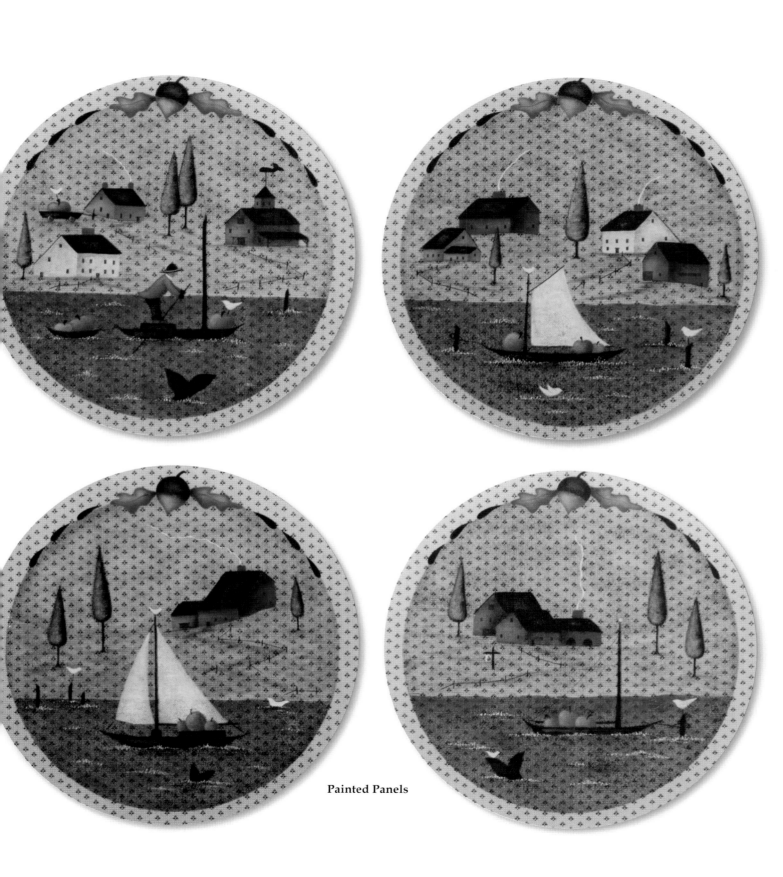

Painted Panels

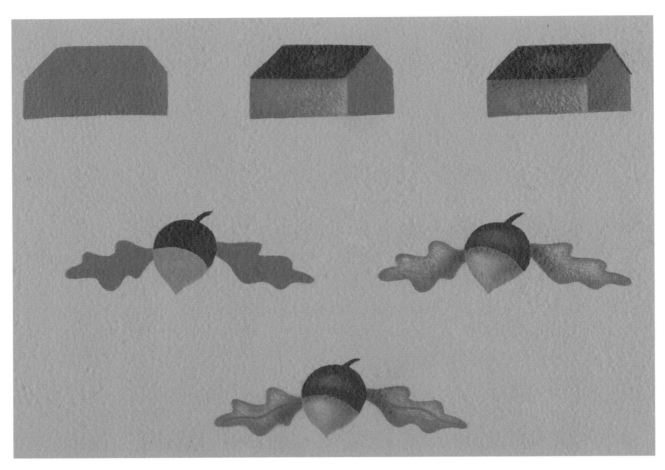

Acorn Cove Worksheet

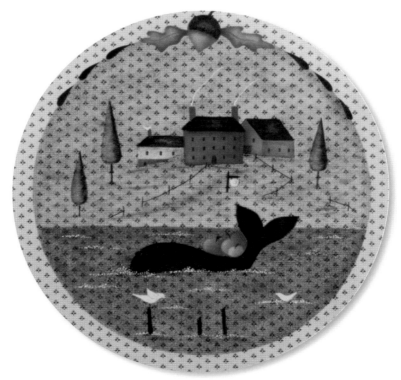

Painted Panel

Quilting

Quilt designed and pieced
by **Cindy Gensamer;**
quilted by **Timeless Treasured Quilts**
on a Statler Stitcher System by Gammill

Skill level: Beginner/Intermediate
Finished block size: 19" x 19"
Finished quilt size: 72" x 72"

Materials

Note: Yardage is based on 42" wide useable fabric.
- Five painted panels trimmed to 13½" x 13½"
- ½ yard navy tonal fabric
- ½ yard green print fabric
- 1 yard mustard tonal fabric (remaining fabric from painting instructions)
- 1½ yards dark red print fabric (includes binding)
- 1¾ yards black paisley fabric
- 80" x 80" piece of backing fabric
- 80" x 80" piece of batting
- Thread in colors to match fabrics
- Basic sewing and rotary cutting supplies

Cutting

From each of the navy tonal and green print, cut:
One 10⅜" x 42" strip; recut into four 10⅜" squares, then cut each square diagonally in half

From the mustard, cut:
Three 10⅜" x 42" strips; recut into twelve 10⅜" squares, then cut each square diagonally in half

From the dark red print, cut:
One 10⅜" x 42" strip; recut into four 10⅜" squares, then cut each square diagonally in half
Fourteen 2½" x 42" strips (for inner border and binding)

From the black paisley, cut:
One 10⅜" x 42" strip; recut into two 10⅜" squares, then cut each square diagonally in half
Eight 6" x 42" strips (for outer border)

Directions

Note: Use a ¼" seam allowance throughout. Sew all pieces with right sides together and raw edges even, using matching thread. Press seams toward the darker fabric unless otherwise indicated.

1. *Center block.* Referring to **Diagram 1**, sew a 10⅜" mustard tonal triangle to each of two opposite sides of one 13½" x 13½" painted panel. Repeat on the other two sides. Square-up to measure 19½" x 19½", making sure the triangle points overlap each other by ¼".

Diagram 1

Diagram 2

2. *Corner blocks.* Following **Diagram 2** and noting color placement, make four 19½" x 19½" blocks using twelve 10⅜" mustard triangles, four 10⅜" black paisley triangles, and the remaining painted panels.

3. *Side sections.* Using 10⅜" triangles, stitch a navy triangle and a green triangle long sides together as shown in **Diagram 3** to make one 10" square. In the same manner, make a green/red square, a mustard/red square, and a mustard/navy square.

Noting orientation and placement, sew the four different color squares together in pairs. Press seams in opposing directions, then sew the pairs together to make one 19½" x 19½" section. Repeat this process to make a total of four sections.

Assembly

1. Referring to the **Quilt Layout Diagram** and noting orientation, sew the center block, corner blocks, and side sections together in three rows of three blocks each. Press row seams in opposing directions, then stitch the rows together to complete the 57½" x 57½" quilt center.

2. *Inner border.* Stitch six 2½" x 42" dark red strips short ends together to make a long strip. Cut two 61½" lengths and two 57½" lengths. Sew shorter strips to the sides of the quilt center, and the longer strips to the top and bottom.

3. *Outer border.* Stitch the 6" x 42" black paisley strips short ends together to make a long strip. Cut two 61½" lengths and two 72½" lengths. Attach to the quilt top in the same manner as the inner border.

4. Layer the quilt top right side up on top of the batting and the wrong side of the backing. Baste the layers together and quilt as desired. Trim the backing and batting even with the quilt top.

5. Bind using the eight 2½" brick strips.

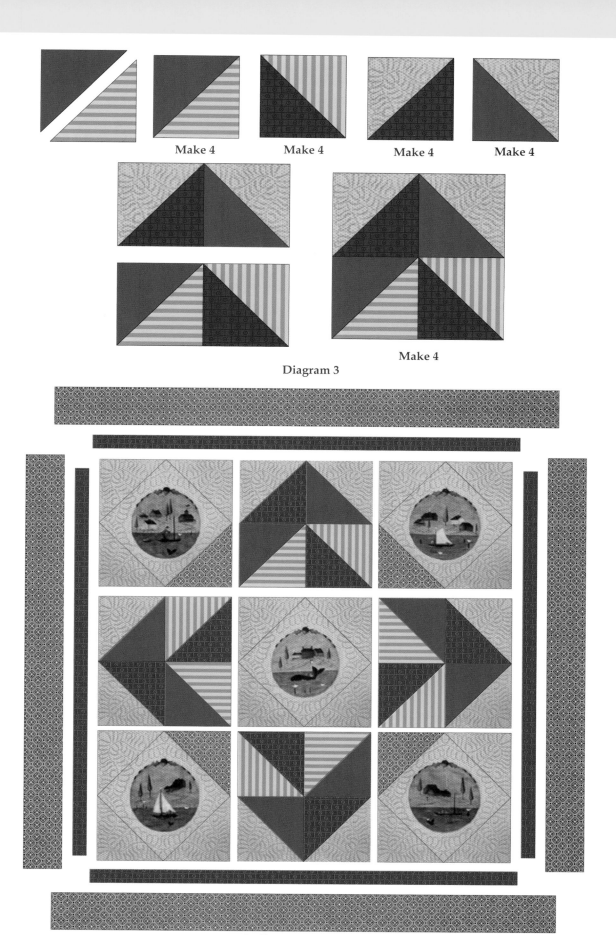

Make 4   Make 4   Make 4   Make 4

Make 4

Diagram 3

Quilt Layout Diagram

Acorn Cove Notion Box

Acorn Cove Quilt Companion Piece

Materials

- *The Quilted Acorn Shoppe* Notion Box
- *DecoArt* Americana Acrylics: Antique Teal, Black Green, Cool Neutral, Honey Brown, Lamp Black, Milk Chocolate, Tangerine, Traditional Burnt Sienna, Traditional Raw Umber
- *Loew-Cornell* LaCornielle Gold Taklon #4 and #6 shader (Series 7300), ¼" angular shader (Series 7400)
- *Scharff Brush Co.* White Bristle #4, #8, and #10 filbert (Series 220); #4 and #6 dome round (Series 245)
- *Silver Brush* 20/0 Ultra Mini Golden Taklon script liner (Series 2407S)
- Brushes of choice: old scruffy brush, ½" soft stencil brush, 2" sponge brush (2)
- *Jo Sonja's* Clear Glaze Medium
- *J.W. etc.* Right-Step Clear Varnish, Matte
- *Miscellaneous:* index card , compass, craft knife*, eraser, freezer paper*, ¼" masking tape, palette knife, paper towels, paper towel and toilet paper tubes, rasp or wood file, ruler, sanding disc, sharp scissors or rotary cutter, small pane of glass*, stylus, tracing paper, transfer paper (gray and white), waxed-paper palette, wood sealer

*Optional

Preparation

1. Remove the thread holder dowel on the wheel. Seal entire box.

2. Load the broad flat side of the 2" sponge brush with Lamp Black. Press brush heavily onto the project surface and lift up, creating a bubbly texture over the outside of the box, lid, and narrow edges of the box (press-and-lift technique). Let dry.

3. Repeat using Honey Brown over the Lamp Black. Start in the desired center of each area, depositing less paint near the edges and at the corners. Leave the narrow edges and the stationary part of the lid with the thread holder Lamp Black. Wash out the brush.

4. Paint the thread dowel and wheel and inside the box Lamp Black.

5. Drybrush the wheel, here and there, with Antique Teal. Drybrush over the Antique Teal with Traditional Burnt Sienna. Let dry.

6. *Distress surface.* Using the rasp, pound all corners and some edges of the box and lid to

flatten them and take away the new, crisp look of the wood. File down some corners of the box and lid to expose bare wood in some areas and Lamp Black in others. Gently distress the thread holder and wheel. Sand all distressed areas smooth and remove dust with a paper towel.

7. *Wood grain.* Mix a glaze of Clear Glaze Medium + Traditional Raw Umber (8:1). Press and lift the glaze onto the box and top of lid, one surface at a time. Let the glaze cover the Honey Brown, but not completely. Use the paper towel tube to roll over the glaze on the lid. Place all fingers across the tube and use light, even pressure as you roll to create the design in the glaze. Repeat on the box sides using a smaller tube. Each surface will be different. Let dry. Use a paper towel to dab a bit of glaze onto any exposed bare wood on the box, lid, and wheel. Let dry.

8. *Transfer pattern.* Position the box lid with the grain of the wood running horizontally. Reduce the quilt square pattern (see Pattern Section) to 55% of the original size.

Trace the pattern and transfer only the circle (a compass will make this easier), the horizon line, and the top edge of the water onto the lid. Place the circle slightly down toward the bottom of the lid to allow for the acorn and leaves at the top.

9. Cut a circle stencil from freezer paper, and tape to the lid for easier painting.

Painting

Note: Drybrush shading and highlights using the dome round brushes. Use with an index card for shading and highlighting the buildings.

Scenes

1. *Sky.* Drybrush sky using Antique Teal. Allow wood grain pattern to show through. Drybrush some small areas of Tangerine through the sky.

2. *Water.* Paint water with Antique Teal, leaving some slight mottling.

3. *Ground.* Paint the ground Milk Chocolate. Highlight the hilltop with Tangerine, and add random Tangerine patches on the ground. Shade with Traditional Raw Umber.

4. *Shading around scene.* Shade all around the inner edge of the circle with Traditional Raw Umber, pulling the color lightly and unevenly into the circle. Shade again closer to the edge with Lamp Black.

5. Transfer the remaining design onto the lid, excluding the details.

6. *Whale.* Base the whale with Lamp Black. Highlight with Tangerine.

7. *Buildings.* Undercoat buildings (left to right) Honey Brown with a Traditional Burnt Sienna foundation, Cool Neutral, and Traditional Burnt Sienna. Highlight all with Tangerine. Shade and add roofs of Lamp Black.

8. *Trees.* All trees are Black Green. Highlight with Tangerine, and shade with Lamp Black. Add Lamp Black trunks.

9. *Shading.* Shade beneath all elements and add Lamp Black paths. Add Lamp Black water and shadows throughout the ground.

10. Remove the paper stencil, and transfer the details onto the scene.

11. *Pylons, sign, gulls, and pumpkins.* Paint the pylons in the water and the signpost with Lamp Black. Shade beneath these using Lamp Black.

The sign is Cool Neutral. Shade lightly with Lamp Black. The gulls are Cool Neutral. Paint the feathery strokes, leaving some Antique Teal showing through. Dab Cool Neutral foam on the water using the tip of a well-loaded script liner.

For pumpkins, add Tangerine to Traditional Burnt Sienna in varying amounts to slightly change the color of each pumpkin. Highlight with Tangerine. Add Lamp Black stems. Paint chimneys Traditional Burnt Sienna, and all doors and windows Lamp Black.

12. *Details.* Define paths with sketchy Lamp Black horizontal lines. Using Lamp Black, paint doorstep, line above barn door, fence lines, right sides of trees, and sign, and attach sign to the post. Chimney smoke is Cool Neutral. Load the scruffy flat brush with Antique Teal, and lightly pounce small bushes throughout the ground.

Acorn and leaves

1. Undercoat the acorn Milk Chocolate, and the cap and stem Lamp Black. Highlight with Tangerine and shade with Lamp Black. Base the leaves with Traditional Burnt Sienna + a touch of Tangerine. Highlight with Tangerine and drybrush a few random areas with Antique Teal. Shade leaves Lamp Black. Cut stencils, or handpaint, the Lamp Black comma strokes.

2. Line the right side of the acorn and undersides of the leaves with Lamp Black thinned slightly with water. Add Traditional Burnt Sienna leaf veins.

Box

1. Drybrush Lamp Black around the wood graining on all edges of the lid and sides using a soft stencil brush. This darkens areas where no black undercoat shows through and nicely frames the wood graining.

2. Where the thread holder is mounted, tape off a ¼" border around the stationary part of the lid. Pounce Traditional Burnt Sienna unevenly into the border, using very little paint and the stencil brush. Remove the tape. Sand lightly so that the border looks slightly worn and faded.

Finishing

1. Erase all transfer lines.

2. Spatter the scene, lid, and the box sides with Lamp Black thinned with water and a stencil brush raked across a palette knife.

3. Finish the box with two coats of matte varnish. Let dry between coats.

Quilt	Approximate Size
Baby Quilt	36" x 54"
Lap Throw	54" x 72"
Twin	54" x 90"
Double	72" x 90"
Queen	90" x 108"
King	108" x 108"

Metric Conversion Chart

1/8" = 3 mm	1" = 2.5 cm	7" = 17.8 cm
1/4" = 6 mm	2" = 5.1 cm	8" = 20.3 cm
1/2" = 1.3 cm	3" = 7.6 cm	9" = 22.9 cm
3/4" = 1.9 cm	4" = 10.2 cm	10" = 25.4 cm
7/8" = 2.2 cm	5" = 12.7 cm	11" = 27.9 mm
	6" = 15.2 cm	12" = 30.5 mm

1/8 yd. = 0.11 m	1/2 yd. = 0.46 m
1/4 yd. = 0.23 m	3/4 yd. = 0.69 m
1/3 yd. = 0.3 m	1 yd. = 0.91 m

Approximate Conversion To Metric Formula

When you know:	Multiply by:			To find:
inches (")	x	25	=	millimeters (mm)
inches (")	x	2.5	=	centimeters (cm)
inches (")	x	0.025	=	meters (m)
feet (' or ft.)	x	30	=	centimeters (cm)
feet (' or ft.)	x	0.3	=	meters (m)
yards (yd.)	x	90	=	centimeters (cm)
yards (yd.)	x	0.9	=	meters (m)

Before beginning, read the directions for the chosen pattern in their entirety. Wash all fabric in the manner in which you intend to wash the finished quilt. This preshrinks the fabric and ensures that it is colorfast. Dry fabric and press to remove wrinkles.

Most fabrics are sold as 44″ wide from selvedge to selvedge, but many vary slightly in width. Fabric width may also change after the fabric is washed. The materials lists and cutting directions in this book are based on a width of at least 42″ of useable fabric after washing and after the selvedges have been trimmed.

Backing fabric and batting dimensions listed are for hand quilting or for quilting on a home sewing machine. Professional quilters using a longarm machine may require a larger backing and batting size. If you intend to have someone else quilt your project, consult them regarding backing and backing size. Cut backing fabric and sew pieces together as necessary to achieve the desired size.

Patterns

The patterns provided for pieced quilts are full size with an included ¼″ seam allowance. The solid line is the cutting line, and the dashed line is the stitching line. A seam allowance is not included on appliqué patterns. Trace all, including any grainline arrows, onto template material.

Marking Fabric Pieces

Test marking pens and pencils for removability before marking pieces for your quilt. If the pattern piece includes a grainline arrow, align the arrow with the fabric grain. Use your marker to trace around the template on the right side of the fabric. Then cut the pieces out.

If you wish to mark the sewing line, use a quilter's ¼″ ruler to measure and mark the seam allowance on the wrong side of the fabric. Mark the pieces needed to complete one block, cut them out, and stitch them together before cutting pieces for the entire quilt.

Trace appliqué patterns lightly on the right side of the fabric or place the templates face down on the wrong side of the fabric. Add the seam allowance specified in the pattern when cutting the fabric pieces out.

Piecing

Set up your machine to sew 12 stitches per inch. If you have not marked the stitching line on fabric pieces, be careful to align fabric edges with the marks on the throat plate of your machine, as necessary, to achieve an accurate ¼″ seam allowance. You can also make a stitching guide in the following way: Place a ruler under the presser foot of the sewing machine aligning the ¼″ marked line on the ruler with the needle. Align a piece of masking tape or a rectangle cut from a moleskin footpad along the right edge of the ruler. Remove the ruler, and place fabric edges against the stitching guide as you sew. Stitch fabric pieces from edge to edge unless directed otherwise in the pattern.

Sew fabric pieces together in the order specified in the pattern. Wherever possible, press seam allowances toward the darkest fabric. When butting seams, press seam allowances in opposing directions.

Fusible Appliqué

This method allows you to complete appliqué very quickly. Follow the directions on the fusible product to prepare and attach appliqué pieces. For most fusible products, it is necessary to flip asymmetrical templates right side down before tracing them on the paper side of the fusible web. Finish the edges of fused appliqué pieces by hand using a blanket stitch or by machine using either a blanket or satin stitch.

Foundation Piecing

Foundation patterns are full size and do not include seam allowances. Trace the foundation patterns onto foundation paper making the number of foundations specified in the quilt pattern. You will piece each foundation in numerical order, placing fabric pieces on the unmarked side of the foundation, then turning the foundation over and stitching on the marked lines. Cut each fabric piece large enough to extend at least ¼" beyond the stitching lines of the section it will cover after it is stitched.

Begin by placing the first fabric piece right side up over section 1 on the unmarked side of the foundation. Hold the foundation up to a light source to better see the marked lines. Place the second piece of fabric right side down over the first piece. Pin fabrics in place if desired. Turn the foundation over and stitch on the line between section 1 and section 2 extending the stitching by two or three stitches on each end of the marked line. Fold the paper foundation along the stitched line so that the seam allowance of the stitched pieces extends beyond the paper. Align the ¼" line of a ruler along the stitches and trim the seam allowance to ¼". Open up the paper, flip the fabric pieces open, and press the unit. Continue adding fabric pieces in the same manner as the second fabric piece until the entire foundation is covered. Trim fabrics ¼" beyond the edges of the foundation. Stitch foundations together as described in the quilt pattern using the paper foundations as a stitching guide. Gently remove foundation paper when instructed to do so in the quilt pattern.

Mitering Border Corners

Fold a border strip in half crosswise to determine the center. Match the center of the border to the center of the quilt, and pin the border to the quilt. Stitch the border to the quilt, beginning and ending exactly ¼" from the quilt edges. Backstitch to secure the stitching at each end. Attach all four borders in the same manner.

Place the quilt right side down on a flat surface, and place one border over the adjacent border as shown. Using a ruler, draw a line at a 45° angle from the inner edge of the uppermost border to the outside edge. Reverse the positions of the borders and repeat to mark a second line. Mark all borders in the same manner.

Pin each set of adjacent borders right sides together along the marked lines. Stitch on the lines from the inner to the outer edge. Backstitch at each edge to secure the seam. Turn the quilt over and check each mitered seam. Trim the seam allowances to ¼".

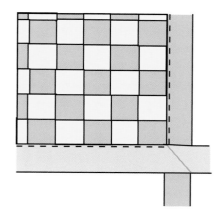

Marking the Quilt Top

Press the quilt top. Test all markers for removability before using them on your quilt. If using a paper design, place it under the quilt top, and trace the design. Use a light source if necessary. If using a stencil, place it on top of the quilt top, and trace the open areas. Use a ruler to mark straight lines such as grids or diagonals that cross fabric pieces.

Masking tape can be used as an alternative to marking straight lines. Place the tape on the quilt where desired and stitch along the edge. Contact paper can be cut into strips and used in the same manner. It can also be cut into other quilting shapes or stencils. Remove tape and contact paper from the quilt top daily to avoid leaving a sticky residue on the quilt.

Basting

The day before you intend to baste the quilt, open up the batting and place it on a flat surface (a bed or carpeted area is ideal). The next day, place the pressed backing fabric wrong side up on a flat, solid surface. Secure the backing in place with masking tape. Smooth the batting on top of the backing. Center the quilt top right side up on the batting.

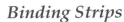

Use a needle and thread in a color that contrasts with the quilt. Baste with large stitches keeping all knots on top of the quilt. Begin in the quilt center and baste first horizontally, then vertically, and finally diagonally to the edge of the quilt top. Also baste at least two rectangles as shown.

To prepare your quilt for quilting on your home sewing machine: Use soluble thread to baste the quilt, or baste using safety pins.

Quilting

Many fine books are available on both hand and machine quilting. Basic hand quilting is described here.

Use quilting thread and a short, strong needle. Place a thimble on the middle finger of your preferred hand. Always begin quilting in the center of the quilt and work your way toward the quilt edge. Make a small knot at the end of the thread, and insert the threaded needle into the quilt top and batting only near where you wish your first quilting stitch to appear. Exit the needle at the beginning of where you want your first visible stitch to be, and gently pop the knot between the fabric fibers into the quilt top.

Begin quilting as follows: Keeping your preferred hand above the quilt and your other hand below it, use your thimbled finger to push the needle straight down through all layers of the

quilt. When you feel the tip of the needle with the index or middle finger of the hand that is below the quilt, use the thumb of your preferred hand to depress the quilt top, and redirect the needle back through the quilt layers to the top of the quilt. Continue in this manner using a rocking motion with your preferred hand. When the thread becomes short, make a small knot at the surface of the quilt top. Then take a stitch and pop the knot into the quilt. Cut the thread where it exits the quilt top. Do not remove basting stitches until quilting is complete.

Binding Strips

Quilts with straight edges can be bound with binding strips cut with the grain of the fabric. Cut binding strips the width specified in the quilt pattern, and sew them together with diagonal seams in the following way: Place two binding strips right sides together and perpendicular to each other, aligning the ends as shown. Mark a line on the top strip, from the upper left edge of the bottom strip to the lower right edge of the top strip, and stitch on the marked line. Trim the seam allowance ¼" beyond the stitching, open up the strips, and press the seam allowance open. When all binding strips have been stitched together, fold the strip in half lengthwise (wrong side in) and press.

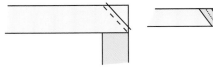

Bias Bindings

Quilts with curved edges must be bound with binding strips cut on the bias. Cut bias strips by aligning the 45° line on a rotary cutting ruler with the bottom edge of the fabric and cutting along the ruler's edge.

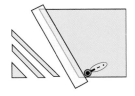

Attaching the Binding

Leaving at least 6" of the binding strip free and beginning several inches away from a corner of the quilt top, align the raw edges of the binding with the edge of the quilt top. Using a standard ¼" seam allowance, stitch the binding to the quilt, stopping and backstitching exactly ¼" from the corner of the quilt top.

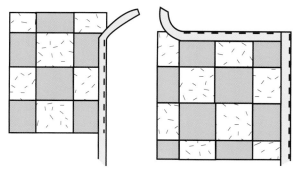

Remove the quilt from the sewing machine, turn the quilt so the stitched portion of the binding is away from you, and fold the binding away from the quilt, forming a 45° angle on the binding. *Hint: When the angle is correct, the unstitched binding strip will be aligned with the next edge of the quilt top.*

Maintaining the angled corner fold, fold the loose binding strip back down, aligning this fold with the stitched edge of the quilt top and the raw edge of the binding with the adjacent quilt top edge. Stitch the binding to the quilt beginning at the fold, backstitching to secure the seam.

Continue attaching the binding in the same manner until you are 6" from the first stitching. Then, fold both loose ends of the binding strip back upon themselves so that the folds meet in the center of the unstitched section of the binding, and crease the folds.

Measure the width of the folded binding strip. Cut both ends of the binding strip that measurement beyond the creased folds. (For example: If the quilt pattern instructed you to cut the binding strips 2½" wide, the folded binding strip would measure 1¼". In this case, you would cut both ends of the binding strip 1¼" beyond the creased folds.)

Open up both ends of the binding strip and place them right sides together and perpendicular to each other as shown. Mark a line on the top strip from the upper left corner of the top strip to the lower right corner of the bottom strip. Pin the strips together and stitch on the marked line.

Refold the binding strip and place it against the quilt top to test the length. Open the binding strip back up, trim the seam allowance ¼" beyond the stitching, and finger press the seam allowance open. Refold the binding strip, align the raw edges with the edge of the quilt top, and finish stitching it to the quilt.

Trim the batting and backing ⅜" beyond the binding stitching. Fold the binding to the back of the quilt, and blind stitch it to the backing fabric covering the machine stitching. Keep your stitches small and close together. When you reach a corner, stitch the mitered binding closed on the back side of the quilt, and pass the needle through the quilt to the right side. Stitch the mitered binding closed on the front side of the quilt, and pass the needle back through the quilt to the back side. Continue stitching the folded edge of the binding to the back of the quilt.

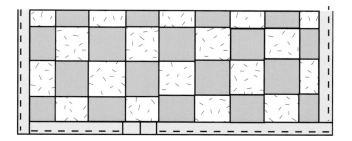

Finishing Your Quilt

Remove all quilt markings. Make a label that includes your name, the city where you live, the date the quilt was completed, and anything else you would like future owners of the quilt to know. Permanent fabric pens make this task easy and allow you to make the label as decorative as desired. Stitch the label to the back of the quilt.

ACRYLIC COLORS
Pigments mixed with polymer emulsion binders, thus, creating a flexible and fast-drying paint film. May be used under, but not over, oil colors.

ALKYD COLORS
Pigments mixed with synthetic alkyd resins, which resemble oil colors and may be mixed with oil colors for faster drying. Must be thinned with odorless thinner or turpentine.

ANTIQUING
Application of a thin glaze of darker color to create an aged appearance with either an antiquing medium or a thin layer of oil paint, which is applied and then wiped away, leaving darkened areas in the corners or grain of the surface.

BASECOAT
Paint applied as a base color before painting a design on the surface.

BLENDING
Mixing wet colors on the painting surface, creating a gradual transition between colors.

BRUSHMIXING
Creating a mixture of colors with the brush as you work, rather than premixing colors with a palette knife.

CHISEL EDGE
The tips of the bristles of a flat or angular brush.

COMMA STROKE
Shape created with a round brush pressed to the surface and then gradually curved as pressure is released and dragged to a fine point.

CORNER-LOAD
Paint loaded onto one corner of a flat brush.

CRACKLING
Creating an aged, distressed finish, usually with a commercial preparation labeled as crackle medium.

C-STROKE (U-STROKE)
Shape created with a flat brush beginning with the chisel of the brush, applying pressure as the brush is pulled into the shape of a C (or U) and then releasing pressure in the second half of the stroke until the brush is once again positioned on the chisel.

DIRTY BRUSH
A brush which has been wiped to remove excess color, but is not totally cleaned.

DISTRESSING
Roughing up a wooden piece to give it an aged, old appearance. Use sandpaper to soften corners and wear paint off the edges of the painted project, or use a hammer, nail, or other tool to create punctures or scratches.

DOTS
Shapes created by dipping the end of a brush, or a stylus into a puddle of paint, then touching the tip to the painting surface. Unless reloaded, the tip will create dots of ever-decreasing size with each touch.

DOUBLE-LOAD
Paint which has been loaded to first one corner of a flat brush and stroked back and forth on the palette to disperse the color, and then corner-loaded with a second color on the other side of the brush and stroked to blend that color across the brush until the two colors meet and evenly blend in the middle of the brush.

DRYBRUSH
A sparse application of unthinned paint, applied with a circular motion and a very light touch. Before painting, most of the paint is first removed from the loaded brush by scrubbing the brush on a paper towel.

ENAMELS
Thin, opaque paint which dries glossy. Most often used on slick surfaces, such as glass.

FAUX FINISH
A false finish. May be any technique which uses paint to make the surface resemble another, such as wood appearing to be marble.

FLOAT
The application of paint with a brush which has been side-loaded with color and stroked on the palette until a smooth transition from color on one side of the brush to no color on the opposite side is achieved. May be used for shading and highlighting.

GEL MEDIUM
Acrylic or oil mediums which make the paint transparent without making it thinner. Some gel mediums may alter the drying time of paint.

GESSO
A common primer for canvas which ma also be used to create smoother wood metal surfaces. May be sanded once dry.

GLAZE
Any application of color made transpare with water or a medium over existing pai

GRAPHITE PAPER (See Transfer Paper)

GOUACHE
Opaque watercolor paint. May contain son acrylic polymer for binding.

HIGHLIGHTS
Areas of white or the lightest color in painting which represent reflected light.

KNEADED ERASER
A pliable, usually gray, eraser whic when "kneaded" or pulled, absorbs exce graphite and presents a clean surface.

LAYER
To apply one color over another. If layers a transparent, new colors will be formed as seen when a layer of blue over yello creates green.

LIFT OUT
The removal of wet paint from the surfa with a brush or tool made damp with wa or other medium.

LINEWORK
Using a wet liner brush evenly loaded w paint and held perpendicular to the surfa to create thin, even-width lines.

LOADING ZONE
Area of paint pulled from the edge of a pa or puddle of color for ease and control loading the brush.

MASKING
Covering an area with commercial maski fluid to protect it from an application paint.

MATTE FINISH
A non-glossy finish.

MEDIUM
A variety of acrylic or oil paint vehic which change the nature or bindi characteristics of the paint, such as maki the paint thinner or more transparent.

IXTURE
vo or more colors mixed together to create
new color.

OPPING
ing a fluffy, soft-haired brush to lightly
ush wet paint to soften or blend the color.

UDDY COLOR
olor mixture which has become dull or
alky because it contains incompatible or
erblended colors.

L COLORS
gments mixed with vegetable (usually
seed) drying oils as a binder, creating a
atively slow-drying, flexible, permanent
int.

PAQUE COLOR
en, streak-free paint coverage which is
ck enough so that no underlying color
ows through.

PEN TIME
e period during which paint remains
orkable before it begins to dry.

UMBLING
ing a slip-slap technique to randomly
nd color.

ALER
protective coating applied between a
rous surface and the basecoat. Prevents
oisture from entering wood surfaces.

ADING
eas of darker value which represent
adows in a painting.

OP TOWELS
avy-duty paper towels which are usually
e in color.

DELOAD
int which has been loaded to one corner
a flat brush, and then stroked back and
th on the palette until the color smoothly
nsitions to no color on the opposite side
the brush. This is usually used to float
or on a surface.

ATTERING
ops of paint scattered on the surface
running the thumb or a palette knife
oss an old toothbrush which has been
ded with paint thinned to an ink-like
nsistency.

SPONGING
Paint applied by tapping the surface with a
damp sponge which has been sparsely
loaded with color.

S-STROKE
Shape created with a flat brush beginning
with the chisel of the brush to create a thin
angled line, applying pressure as the brush
is pulled perpendicular to the line, and then
releasing pressure as the brush is once again
positioned on the chisel and pulled at an
angle to form an S.

STIPPLING
Paint applied by tapping the surface with a
stipple brush, or old, worn brush, which has
been scantly loaded with paint from the side
of the paint puddle.

STROKEWORK
The use of specialized brushstrokes of
varying pressure and direction of the brush
to create painted designs.

STYLUS
A metal tool with a dull point used with
transfer paper to transfer design patterns to
a surface.

TACK CLOTH
Lint-free cloth used to remove dust from
surfaces of dust before painting or varnish-
ing. May be microfiber or commercially
treated cheesecloth.

TEARDROP STROKE
An uncurved and elongated comma stroke.

THINNER
Liquid used to reduce the thickness of paint.
May be water for watercolor, water or
specialized mediums for acrylic paints, or
odorless thinner or turpentine for oils.

TRANSFER PAPER
Thin paper coated on one side with graphite
or chalk used between the pattern and the
surface with pressure on a stylus to transfer
the pattern lines to the surface. Comes in
gray (graphite), white, yellow, blue, or red.

TRANSPARENT COLOR
A coating of paint which allows underlying
paint layers to show through.

UNDERCOAT
An opaque application of color under an
area of a design.

VALUE
The relative measure of how light or dark
a color is.

VARNISH
A sealer applied over a painted surface to
protect it. Varnish may be gloss, semigloss
(satin), or matte.

WALKING COLOR
Enlarging an area of color by reapplying
the color several times in overlapping
applications. Often used with floating color.

WASH
Ink-like consistency paint which creates a
transparent layer of color while allowing the
base color to show through.

WATERCOLORS
Pigments mixed with natural gums as a
binder which are transparent in nature.

WET-INTO-DRY
An application of wet paint onto a dry
surface. Generally a watercolor term.

WET-INTO-WET
Applying wet paint into an area already wet
with paint, water, or medium to create a
blended look.

WET PALETTE
A variety of palettes which keep acrylic
paint wet and workable in the palette. Paint
may be placed on wet shop towels, synthetic
chamois with deli-wrap on top, or a sponge
with commercial wet palette paper on top.
When paper is used, it must be porous
enough to allow moisture to wick into the
paint.

Trudy A. Beard
Trudy Beard Designs
386-788-6831
4256 Mayfair Lane
Port Orange, FL 32129
www.trudybearddesigns.com
trudy@trudybearddesigns.com

Ronnie Bringle
Country Friends
620-632-4218
1345 W 530th
McCune, KS 66753
www.ronniebringle.com
ronniebringle@ckt.net

Lynne Deptula
Distinctive Brushstrokes
616-940-1899
7245 Cascade Wds Dr SE
Grand Rapids, MI 49546
www.distinctivebrushstrokes.com
dbrush1@aol.com

Judy Diephouse
Distinctive Brushstrokes
616-874-1656
9796 Myers Lake Ave
Rockford, MI 49341
www.distinctivebrushstrokes.com
distinctj@aol.com

Donna Dewberry
Dewberry Crafts
352-394-7344
9006 Mossy Oak Lane
Clermont, FL 34711
www.dewberrycrafts.com

Cynthia Erekson
Quilted Acorn Shoppe
978-462-0974
72 Newburyport Turnpike
Newbury, MA 01951
www.quiltedacorn.com
info@quiltedacorn.com

Chris Thornton-Deason
Chris Thornton Designs
316-253-5442
PO Box 617
Douglass, KS 67039
www.christhorntondesigns.com
chris@christhorntondesigns.com

Peggy Harris
Peggy Harris Collectibles
615-382-2050
3848 Martins Chapel Road
Springfield, TN 37172
www.peggyharris.com
peggy@peggyharris.com

Jo Sonja Jansen
Jo Sonja's
707-445-9306
2136 Third Street
Eureka, CA 95501
www.josonja.net
folk@josonja.com

Andy Jones
*Decorative Arts
Collection Museum*
404-627-3662
650 Hamilton Ave., S.E.
Suite M
Atlanta, GA 30312
www.decorativeartscollection.org
andyjones@decorativeartscollection.org

Sherry Nelson
The Magic Brush
520-558-2285
PO Box 16530
Portal, AZ 85632-0530
www.sherrynelson.com
birdlady@sherrycnelson.com

Jamie Mills-Price
Between The Vines
541-863-7933
P O Box 278
129 NE First AV
Myrtle Creek, OR 97457
www.betweenthevines.com
jamie@betweenthevines.com

Peggy Stogdill
574-633-4689
12750 Kern Road
Mishawaka, IN 46544
www.peggystogdill.com
painting@peggystodgill.com

Bobbie Takashima
Country Keepsakes
619-474-3768
340 W 26th St "C"
National City, CA 91950
www.bobbieartstudio.com
btfrogs@aol.com

Mary M. Wiseman
Mary's Publications
586-264-7328
12856 Whitfield
Sterling Heights, MI 48312
www.marywiseman.com
mwis459337@aol.com